THE PRAYING CHURCH MADE SIMPLE

A Strategy for Congregational Transformation to 'A House of Prayer'

The Process

P. Douglas Small

The Praying Church Made Simple

A Strategy for Congregational Transformation to 'A House of Prayer'

The Process

ISBN: 978-0-9975802-7-3

Published by Alive Publications
a division of
Alive Ministries: PROJECT PRAY
PO Box 1245

Kannapolis, NC 28082

www.alivepublications.org
www.projectpray.org

PREFACE

This is not meant to replace the earlier book, *Transforming Your Church into a House of Prayer,* or *The Praying Church Resource Guide* with their numerous practical resources, but to be a simpler lens through which one might approach the process and begin the journey of bringing prayer to the center of congregational life.

The purpose of this resource is to simplify the transformational process in those earlier writings; to establish clear beginning points for the revitalizing prayer effort; and to set forth a simpler approach to prayer mobilization for the smaller congregation.

This book and its companion will be greatly increased if it sits in the context of the Prayer Leaders Continuing Education process. Consider starting a learning group with other churches in your area. Join the Prayer Trainer's Network. Check out the resources at www.projectpray.org or at www.alivepublications.org.

 First printing, November, 2011.

Contents

THE PROCESS

START THE CHURCH PRAYING

MILESTONE ONE
LAUNCH A CHURCH-WIDE PRAYER MEETING

DEVELOP LEADERS

PERSONAL PRAYER

Contents

PERSPECTIVES

(digital files on disc)

The idea of the Praying Church is so simple!

THE CHURCH

There cannot be a Praying Church without ***a prayer meeting*** – not a preaching or teaching meeting, at least, not primarily, but a gathering of the church to engage God prayerfully, beyond personal prayer requests, for missional purposes, to wait on the Lord, to hear from heaven.

Stewarded (prayer leadership) plus the two big cogs that drive the entire process: At-home prayer and the church gathered for prayer.

DEVELOPING LEADERS

Prayer must be stewarded. The altar had to be maintained – the wood cut and cured, stacked and fed to the fire, the sacrifices prepared and laid on the altar, the fire stoked and sustained. The law of the altar was, "The fire shall ever be burning, it shall never go out." Leaders lead by example – praying at-home and at-church.

PERSONAL, AT-HOME PRAYER

You can never have a praying church if people are only praying at-church. The recovery of daily personal character-building prayer is critical, as is the family altar. Less than ten-percent of pastors and laity pray with their spouses and families. If you have people of prayer, you will always have a house of prayer.

The praying church is simple – as simple as a simple, single cell. And that, we know now, is not simple at all. One gram of DNA can contain the equivalent amount of data to 1 trillion CDs. The simple cell is incredibly complex – and so is the church, as a house of prayer, for in it, in prayer, in the experience and workings of prayer, are found the DNA of the church itself.

The Praying Church Made Simple represents the first three *Milestones* on the journey to transform the culture of the church.

Out of 'Seven Markers' of a praying church, the three first simple steps are:

- Learning leaders.
- The church in prayer.
- Daily, personal prayer.

Introduction

Two decades ago, I backed into the international prayer movement. The first ten years I spent as a representative of International Renewal Ministries, an outreach of Multnomah Bible College and Seminary, and their effort to call pastors to prayer. In those days, I served twelve states in the pastoral prayer movement, in dozens of cities, where extended prayer times, called 'Pastoral Prayer Summits' were conducted with pastors from diverse denominational backgrounds.

In the next decade, my denomination, the Church of God, transitioned me from a national teaching evangelist, working under the auspices of the General Evangelism Department, to a consultant on prayer ministries. I began conducting training sessions for local churches and their prayer teams. The focus of these multi-church, prayer-leader gatherings was to develop the church as a 'house of prayer.'

In that season, I wrote the book *Transforming Your Church into a House of Prayer.* That book provided a conceptual construct but it lacked practical 'how to' materials. *(Transforming Your Church into a House of Prayer - Revised Edition* is available at www.alivepublications.org.)

The need for practical materials and, more specifically, a process for helping a congregation recover Christ-centered, transformational prayer was clear. Inevitably, I was asked, "Do you have resources for this – or that?" At times, I would be aware of ready resources, and at other times, I attempted to create them. I was in the constant mode of finding or creating special resources for *individual* congregations.

The greatest need is for materials related to the single-cell church of less than 100 members. After some years, we created the *Praying Church Resource Guide,* loaded with practical helps. The response to that 700-page loose-leaf guide filled with practical helps for prayer ministry was, *"That is too much!"* What do you do? Too little; too much!

The Praying Church Made Simple is my answer. It offers a simple 1-2-3 step process, rich with support and learning materials, designed to aid a small congregation in a quick, but studied, launch of their prayer effort. More than a book, *The Praying Church Made Simple* is a leader's guide for a multi-year process to create a culture of prayer in a congregation. Here, you will find a strategy to lay the groundwork for an effective prayer ministry. It is designed as a companion to the *Praying Church Resource Guide,* and also, the book *Transforming Your Church into a House of Prayer - Revised Edition.* For some, those resources, though full of practical helps, was too daunting. This simplifies the process – I hope!

The challenge of how to make the transition from a house of praise and preaching to a house of prayer, without displacing either praise or preaching, is not simple. It is not single-dimensional. It is not a mere matter of more prayer activity. It is, in fact, quite complex – multi-faceted. How can prayer or prayer ministry be anything but simple? The problem is that we narrow prayer – to: 'a little talk with Jesus,' 'a chat with a friend,' 'spiritual warfare,' 'the verbalization of our faith,' 'meditation' – and more. If you focus on prayer as *activity at the church,* and fail to address *personal prayer and the recovery of the family altar,* your efforts will fail. You will never have a praying church without praying people and praying homes.

We begin with a SIMPLE THREE-STEP PROCESS. These are the most strategic beginning points in the journey. They are three of the 'Seven Markers of a Praying Church.' In this book, you will find supplemental materials which include:

DISCOVERY MOMENTS – Additional recommended learning options which point to files included in *PERSPECTIVES,* on the enclosed disc. Videos are included on the enclosed disc or can also be accessed online at www.youtube.org/user/projectpray.

GROUP TALK – Questions and statements to promote for group discussion.

ACTION STEPS – Opportunities to process the material in a practical manner. These action steps build toward the completion of the Progress Markers – the Milestones in your journey.

PROGRESS MARKERS – These, when accomplished, are 'milestones' in your progress toward becoming a house of prayer.

Also, you will greatly benefit from this process if you are a part of a Prayer Leader's Continuing Education effort, a quarterly gathering of pastors and prayer leaders, led by a PROJECT PRAY certified trainer, using the PLCE materials available from www.alivepublications.org.

There are three principal progress indicators about which are recorded in this book. They are:

1. The launch of the successful church-wide prayer meeting;
2. The identification and development of a small group of potential prayer leaders-learners;
3. The practice of persistent daily personal prayer by the people, but in the beginning, principally by the pastors, prayer leaders and those engaged in regular congregational prayer.

DISCOVERY MOMENTS help address the underlying presuppositions. They answer the *'why'* of what you are doing. If you can engage the practices, but fail to understand *why* you do what you do, the prayer ministry will ultimately fail.

The ACTION STEPS give you an opportunity to explore, to flesh out the *whys*. They will test the resolve and the unity of your prayer team as you engage the ideas and practices. They will move you toward the completion of the *Milestones* that will serve as progress markers for the journey.

Here is the recommendation.

READ THIS BOOK TWICE

1. First, read *The Praying Church Made Simple, A Strategy for Congregational Transformation* . (Don't worry about the bonus volume, *PERSPECTIVES*. Get your head around the idea of the 'three simple *practices.')* Don't take the Action Steps. Ignore the Discovery Moments. Read past the Progress Markers.
2. Then, ***REREAD*** the book, stopping to take in all the corollary material included in *PERSPECTIVES* (Volume 2).
    - Engage in the Discovery Moments: Watch the videos and read the corollary materials, etc.
    - Complete the Action Steps.
    - You are the scout, and once you understand the concept and have reviewed the corollary support materials, you will be better prepared to lead your prayer pioneers on a journey toward becoming a 'house of prayer.'
3. Now you are ready ***TO TRAIN*** with this material in mind. Lay out a plan to take your prayer learning team through the material. Once a month with potential prayer leaders seems a reasonable pace. Remember, your goal is not 'head' knowledge, but 'heart' knowledge; and, you are implement-

ing as you move forward. So, monthly prayer leader's training allows time to process the material and also implement the ideas. You want to get this book into the hands of your potential leaders early in the process. Encourage them to do as you did – read, re-read this volume. Then, explore all the action steps, the discovery moments, the milestones. Then, learn together with everyone having had a glimpse of where you are going.

4. Make sure you are not only ***learning together,*** but also ***praying together*** and, of course, leading prayer together.

What, How and Why!

The book of Proverbs often features the triad of *knowledge, understanding, and wisdom.*

- Knowledge answers 'what' questions;
- Understanding answers 'how' questions;
- Wisdom answers 'why' questions.

You want prayer leaders who know *what* to do, now and later. They must also be leaders who know *'how'* to execute their role in prayer ministry leadership and, more importantly, *'why'* they are doing what they are doing.

As you pray and learn together, your *vision* for prayer ministry will grow and expand. You want it to develop. The tendency is to move too quickly, from an underdeveloped *vision* to *tactical implementation.* That is, you find some idea, some prayer program that you implement immediately. It may be a six-week program or a six-month program. Such tactical event type experiences are helpful. It is not that they hurt your process. Rather, they derail the strategic, undergirding transformational aspect of your effort. They are tangible and measurable, more so than your strategic thinking and planning. In the end, they deliver less long-term change than they do when they rise out of a strategic plan. Eventually you will discover that mere prayer activities, one or two prayer programs and a few prayer tools, cannot sustain your prayer effort. They are inadequate because they do not address all of your prayer needs. You need more than prayer tools or tactics, more than a program. You need a prayer *strategy*, a holistic approach, and that demands macro-thinking and planning. If your *vision* is too narrow – "Let's just get people praying, let's mobilize intercessors, let's have a school of prayer, let's prayer walk the community," etc. – then you leap from *vision* into a *tactical aspect* of what should be included in a larger *strategy*. You want to move not from *vision* to *tactics*, but from *vision*, through *strategy*, to the *tactical*.

Using one prayer tactic/program without knowing how that prayer tool is to be partnered with another, without seeing *how* the parts fit together, will make your effort too narrow, too one-dimensional for long-term success. Utilizing a single component of prayer, one program or tool, though valuable, is rarely enough to sustain a broad movement of prayer.

The difference between *strategy* and *tactics* is simply this: *tactics* are the individual pieces, the parts, the components, in this case, of your prayer process; but *strategy* is how those parts fit together, why one is foundational for another, how they relate. *Vision* is the big picture; *strategy* is the big picture plan; and *tactics* are the rollout, piece-by-piece and step-by-step. You will not see the whole vision in the beginning, nor will you have a complete strategy – vision and strategy will grow. Still, you do want a larger perspective than you currently have; some sense of where you are ultimately going. Begin with micro-strategies, and grow them into a multi-year, macro-strategy.

LET'S START THE JOURNEY.

PHILIPPIANS 2, The Message

If you've gotten anything at all out of following Christ, if his love has made any difference in your life, if being in a community of the Spirit means anything to you, if you have a heart, if you care – then do me a favor: Don't push your way to the front; don't sweet-talk your way to the top. Put yourself aside, and help others get ahead. Don't be obsessed with getting your own advantage. Forget yourselves long enough to lend a helping hand (v. 1-4).

Think of yourselves the way Christ Jesus thought of himself. He had equal status with God but didn't think so much of himself that he had to cling to the advantages of that status no matter what. Not at all. When the time came, he set aside the privileges of deity and took on the status of a slave, became human! Having become human, he stayed human. It was an incredibly humbling process. He didn't claim special privileges. Instead, he lived a selfless, obedient life and then died a selfless, obedient death – and the worst kind of death at that – a crucifixion (vs. 5-8).

Because of that obedience, God lifted him high and honored him far beyond anyone or anything, ever, so that all created beings in heaven and on earth – even those long ago dead and buried – will bow in worship before this Jesus Christ, and call out in praise that he is the Master of all, to the glorious honor of God the Father (vs. 9-11).

The Pharisee taught us that prayer alone, the act of prayer, is not adequate unless it has about it the right attitude, the right spirit! Nothing will enable your process more, or sabotage it, perhaps fatally, than a failure to grasp the 'spirit' of this passage (Luke 18).

Seven Markers of a Praying Church

1. Led by ***a praying pastor, aided by a prayer leadership team***, we commit to bring prayer to the heart of all we do!
2. We will encourage ***at-home, daily, Jesus-be-Jesus-in-me praying.*** We will reestablish our personal and family altars.
3. We will call our congregation to ***regular prayer,*** with the goal of establishing a regular weekly prayer meeting for the entire church.
4. We will honor those who carry a special calling to pray – ***intercessors.*** We will identify intercessors, encourage them, train them, team them, deploy them and debrief them.

5. We will ***engage in prayer evangelism, turning prayer outward*** onto the neighborhood, the city, state and nation, and we will adopt a mission field for prayer, one near and one far.
6. We will ***offer regular training in the area of prayer*** – for our people, leaders, intercessors, prayer evangelism, our youth and children, our families.
7. We will ***work toward the creation of a prayer room or center,*** a physical space dedicated to prayer at our church, and we will encourage the use of such a space by members and prayer groups.

Ten Prayer Values

What we believe, and how we behave:

- **We value prayer;** *therefore, we will feature prayer in our worship and make prayer a central element of all ministry.*
- **We are a praying people;** *therefore, we will nurture at-home daily prayer,* family prayer, husband-wife, parent-child prayer connections, providing resources, training and nudging new and old Christians to deepen their prayer lives.
- **We believe that we are a kingdom of priests** and that prayer and worship is our highest calling, and that as priests, we are not only recipients of blessing, but the conveyors of blessing; *therefore, in prayer, we commit to pray for the favor and blessing of God upon others;* for protective care, upon our pastor, the church staff, the church family, our city and our nation. *We bless,* we do not curse. We ask God not for what we deserve, but for blessing – for continued grace and mercy!
- **We value holiness and righteousness** as the mark of God upon a people, and we recognize that the church desperately needs revival and our nation needs a great awakening; *therefore, we regularly and consistently cry out to God for revival in the church and a great awakening* for our nation.
- **We believe in the power of petition,** that God answers when people pray rightly; *therefore, we faithfully take the needs of the church, one another, the city and the world before the throne of God and ask for grace!* We provide a means whereby requests for prayer are taken seriously and held up in prayer persistently, beseeching God expectantly for an answer.
- **We believe in the power of God through intercession;** *therefore, we identify, train, team and mobilize intercessors* for the under-girding of the ministries of the Church, and for the support of the various mission endeavors of the congregation.
- **We believe that prayer is essential to the success of every endeavor,** that without Him we can do nothing, and whatever we do in His behalf without dependence upon Him is less than it

might have been, given dependence in prayer; *therefore, our rule is no one works unless someone prays!*

- **We believe that the reception of the gospel unto salvation is a spiritual issue;** *therefore, we pray for the harvest,* that blind eyes will be open to the gospel, ears will be enabled to hear and receive the truth of Christ, hearts may be receptive to the good news that goes forth in power out of prayer.
- **We believe that there is a definitive connection between prayer and the harvest;** *therefore, we insist that prayer must have a missional dimension,* that we must pray for lost loved ones, for the unreached in our city and the world.
- **We believe, "God governs the world by the prayers of His people;"** *therefore, we pray for our city, state and national leaders.* We pray about world conditions and various global crises. We invite God's intervening reign. We pray, *"Thy Kingdom come, thy will be done."*

ACTION STEP: Complete the Rating Sheet: Ten Prayer Values.

START THE CHURCH PRAYING

CHAPTER 1

The Seven Markers of a Praying Church

Jesus said, *"My house shall be a house of prayer for the nations!"*

1. Led by ***a praying pastor, aided by a prayer leadership team***, we commit to bringing prayer to the heart of all we do! *"Without Christ, we can do nothing!"* Without prayer, we fail to invite Him into the process. Therefore, our resources – spiritual and material – our plans and programs, we will bathe in prayer.

2. We will encourage ***at-home, daily, Jesus-be-Jesus-in-me praying.*** We will reestablish personal and family altars. We will embrace the discipline of daily time with God, with one another as couples, and as families, until daily prayer is a delight, and we take joy in spending private time with God. We will champion the idea of personal prayer rooms/closets.

3. We will call our congregation to ***regular prayer,*** with the goal of establishing a regular weekly prayer meeting for the entire church. We will make the prayer meeting as important as Sunday morning singing and preaching. We will emphasize special days of prayer. We will lace prayer into the fabric of the Sunday worship service. We want a pervasive movement of prayer, not merely prayer activities. Eventually, we will offer numerous ways to connect in prayer – prayer groups, prayer chains, embedded intercessors for various ministries and more.

The Praying Church Made Simple – the first three of the 'Seven Markers of a Praying Church.' 1. A praying pastor with praying prayer leaders. 2. At-home personal and family prayer. 3. The church at prayer.

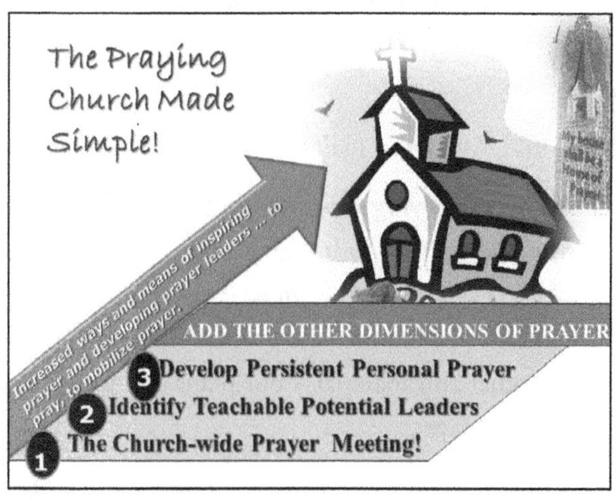

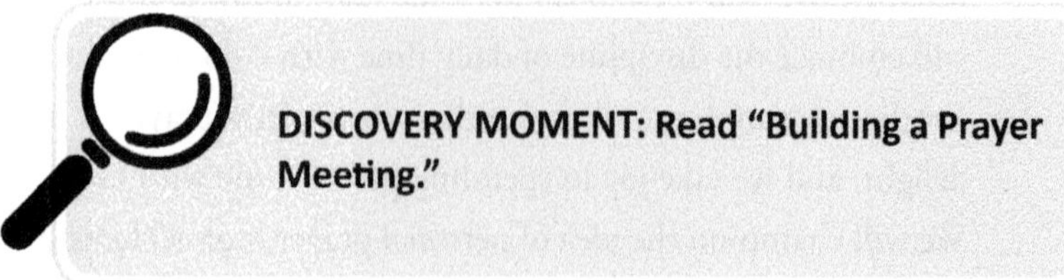

Three Markers

The first three markers constitute 'the three-legged stool' of 'the Praying Church Made Simple:'

1. Leaders who pray.
2. People who pray at home.
3. A church that prays together.

Begin by ***calling the church to prayer*** and by offering a time for them to gather for prayer.

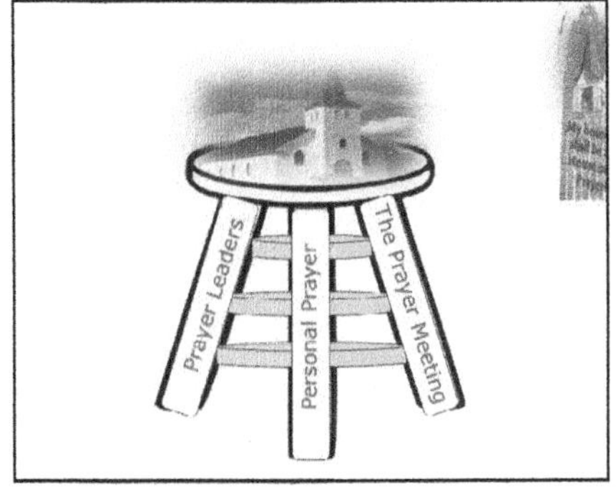

- From among those who respond, ***look for teachable potential praying leaders.***
- During your congregational prayer gathering, and among your developing prayer leaders, ***encourage daily personal prayer,*** with an eye toward the family altar, and beyond that, a culture of Christ-sensitivity in the home.
- To have ***a praying church*** demands ***a praying people.***
- And it demands ***leaders who exemplify prayer***. That makes daily time with God as a critical non-negotiable.

These three,
personal prayer,
corporate prayer
and developing leaders,
out of the seven markers, are the primary
first steps in launching a prayer effort.

ADDITIONAL MARKERS OF A PRAYING CHURCH

4. We will honor those who carry a special calling to pray – ***intercessors.*** We will identify intercessors, encourage them, train them, team them, deploy them and debrief them. But we will not confine the intercessory ministry to this team; rather, we will see them as models for prayer, as those with white-hot hearts whom God has called to be at the hidden forefront of spiritual beachheads we are called to claim. We want a spirit of intercession to grip our entire church, a spirit of prayer – and particularly, prayer for others, selfless prayer, prayer for the lost, prayer for the nations, prayer for spiritual awakening!

5. We will ***engage in prayer evangelism, turning prayer out ward*** onto the neighborhood, the city, state and nation, and we will adopt a mission field for prayer, one near and one far. We will pray for the harvest. We will seek to identify the people for whom God has made us most responsible, and we will begin the process of evangelism in prayer, look for ways to care, and steward the opportunities to share the gospel. We will employ the strategy of the 'three greats' – we will pray, care and look for opportunities to share the good news.

6. We will ***offer regular training in the area of prayer*** – for our people, leaders, intercessors, prayer evangelism, our youth and children, our families.

7. We will ***work toward the creation of a prayer room or center,*** a physical space dedicated to prayer at our church, and we will encourage the use of such a space by members and prayer groups. We will provide resources for prayer that run

through all our departments, until we have a praying church and not merely a prayer ministry.

- *The **goal** of a praying church is first to create a core group of people committed to prayer, with an initial goal to enroll 20% of its membership in some aspect of the prayer process.*
- *The **focus** is on changing the habits of the people.*
- *At-home prayer and at-church regular prayer meetings are the two big cogs that drive the prayer process.*
- *Eventually, the regular church-wide prayer event should spawn prayer groups (7 for each 100 members). These prayer groups (composed of 3-12 individuals each) operate around a specific focus for prayer! (Life-effectiveness is 6-18 months.)*
- *PIT crews (personal intercessory support teams for the ministry leaders and departments) should also be considered.*
- ***It takes 3-5 years to affect the culture of a church! Don't give up!***

DISCOVERY MOMENT: Watch the video "Reviewing the Seven Markers."

ACTION STEP: Reread the Seven Markers, then complete the Seven Markers Rating Sheet. Have each member of your team do so.

Four Dimensions Inside the Seven Markers

Throughout this book, you will find the concept of the 'four dimensions' of prayer ministry – they are four of the seven markers. Inside the four dimensions are the two big cogs that drive the entire process – at-home daily prayer and pervasive prayer throughout church life, anchored by the church-wide prayer meeting. The two big cogs, along with the mobilization of intercessors and a prayer evangelism interface, constitute the four dimensions.

Each of these four dimensions is a world of prayer, a sphere of prayer. You want to integrate into your effort a balanced theology of prayer. In earlier books and seminars, I have emphasized Paul's theology of prayer (1 Tim. 2:1), where he delineates four aspects of prayer – supplications (prayer requests, petitions), prayer (literally, worship, to turn one's face toward God. That is the heart of prayer, worshipful communion with God), intercession (to meet God, as king, on behalf of another), and thanksgiving. Communion with God is at the heart of prayer. The *relationship* grants the *right* of petition and the *responsibility* of intercession. All of these – communion, petition and intercession – are to be unwrapped in an attitude of gratitude. Develop these, in balance, and you will have a healthy, vital and powerful prayer effort and a vibrant congregation.

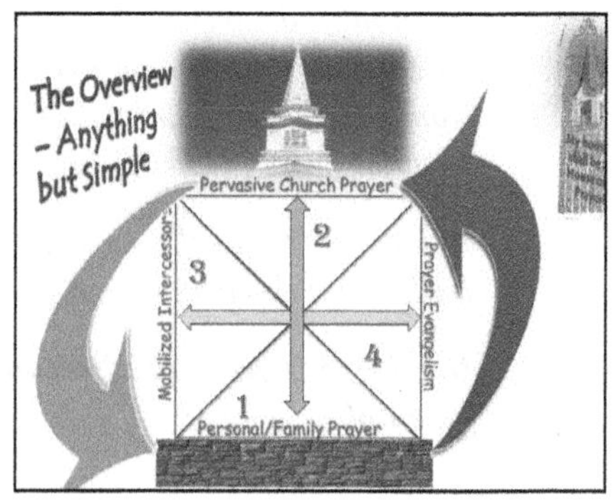

At-home prayer focuses on the *face* of God, our relationship with the Father, in Christ, out of His finished work of the cross, possible by the enabling Spirit, over an open Bible. It is about being personally transformed, about knowing God.

At-church prayer implores His *hand* on all we do, His anointing on the ministries of the church, and does so without omitting our corporate need to seek the *face* of God. The church prayer meeting is, as is our daily time with God, a declaration of church-wide dependence. It is prayer from the 'office' of the church, plural prayer, prayers of agreement. Nothing will promote harmony and invite God's power and blessing more than humility and unity – *"Without Him, we can do nothing."* It is humility before His holiness that creates a climate of repentance and brokenness before God. Then, prayer brings us to faith and obedience. To unity and agreement. To discernment and unified, collaborative engagement. It sensitizes us to the energizing power of the Spirit at work in our midst and our need to consider the incomplete mission before us and ongoing character development within us.

Intercessory prayer allows us to see with the *eyes* of God. It involves insight we could know in no other way. Here, spiritual perception is heightened. We see as God sees. Disclosures come forth. Clarity emerges. God's secrets are unwrapped. Intercession has both a priestly and prophetic dimension. It involves hearing and seeing. It is, at times, a believer – indeed, a congregation – before God on behalf of another, perhaps even a city or a nation. At other times, it is the intercessor praying into and over some need – a person, a place or an issue – and pleading for the will of God to be done, the Word of God to be perceived and believed. Indeed, it is prayer for God to enforce His will.

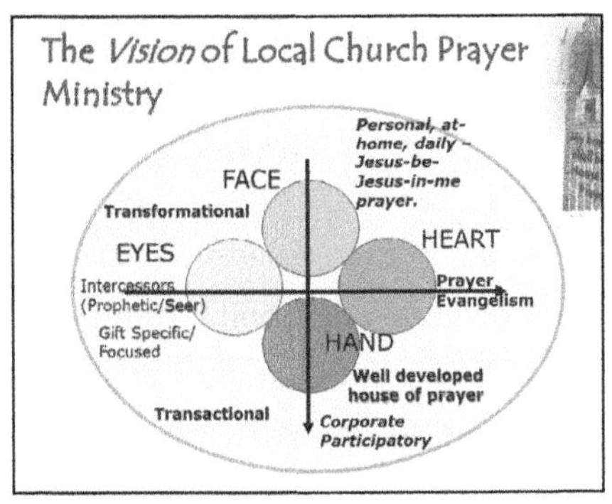

Prayer evangelism is the *heart* of God, a heart for the lost, for those disconnected from a relationship with Him. These four dimensions are key to balance and breadth. Without prayer evangelism, your prayer focus is internal. You are failing to adequately connect prayer and mission. Without at-home prayer, you lack integrity in your prayer effort. Secret, closet prayer is a fundamental partner to public prayer. Without corporate prayer, the church itself lacks power.

Without intercessors, your prayer effort lacks a certain intensity and depth. Shallow praying yields little results. Four dimensions in two pairs – at-home and at-church prayer; intercession and prayer evangelism.

DISCOVERY MOMENT: Read the "Four Dimensions of a Congregational Prayer Ministry" and watch the video "The Four-Dimension Model."

From Seven Markers to Three Simple Practices

Prayer tends to shrink to the boundaries of our own self-interests and preferences. And when it does, it dries up. God desires to expand us, stretch us and grow us, and that happens most profoundly in our prayer encounters with Him. To support a broad prayer effort, you need a means by which you can consistently, graciously expose believers to a world of prayer and needs beyond their comfort zone.

So, eventually, a prayer room or center, a prayer corner in the sanctuary, or even a sign-up counter in the foyer, will serve as visible space dedicated to keeping your prayer effort before the people.

Ongoing training aims to expose the people of the congregation systematically to the various aspects of all four dimensions. You might consider a study or leading a series on prayer, but primarily focus your training on developing a prayer leadership team.

The leadership team is necessary to guide the prayer process. They cannot be apart from it or above it. They cannot merely direct it. They must be immersed in the prayer effort – praying *at home* and *at church,* embracing the call to *intercession* and *prayer evangelism.*

These are the four critical dimensions:

1. Personal-family prayer;
2. The church at prayer;

3. Mobilized intercessors;
4. Prayer evangelism.

Together, with prayer leaders, on-going training and a prayer room/center, they constitute the Seven Markers of a Praying Church.

In this *Praying Church Made Simple* model, you will focus primarily on the first three of the seven markers – developing prayer leaders; encouraging personal, daily, at-home prayer; and the congregational prayer meeting.

The Two Big Cogs Inside the Seven Markers

Of the seven markers of the praying church, the two most critical components are...

<u>at-home</u>, daily praying and...

...the <u>church-wide</u> prayer effort...

...which gives impetus to the church as a house of prayer.

At-home and at-church, back and forth. These two feed each other. It is difficult to say which of these is the more critical. At-church, corporate praying cannot take the place of personal prayer; and personal prayer cannot fulfill the function of corporate prayer. In the gospels, we find Jesus in private prayer headed for the cross; in Acts, the Church is constituted out of a corporate prayer gathering in the Upper Room, in which the Spirit baptizes and energizes. Compelled, both together and personally,

they publically give witness to the resurrection, the ascension and the enthronement of Christ. The book of Acts is the story of a praying Church – from Jerusalem to Rome. And yet, the emphasis on the corporate is not without glimpses of personal prayer. Here, we find a balance – the corporate and the personal.

The Gospels – In the gospels, we find the personal prayer life of Jesus. He prayed early in the morning. While it was still dark, he left the house and went to a solitary place, where he prayed (Mk. 1:35). In Matthew 14:23, he chose solitude again, and went on a mountainside to pray at the close of the day. In Luke 6:12, he spent the night alone in prayer. In the garden of Gethsemane, he removed himself for the sake of privacy, and knelt down, and prayed (Luke 22:41-44). He prayed alone often (Luke 5:16), and he prayed fervently *"with loud cries and tears"* (Heb. 5:7).

In Matthew, the prayer life of Jesus is noted twenty-one times, thirteen in Mark, twenty-five in Luke and six in John's gospel. Some of these, given the nature of the synoptic gospels, are different accounts of the same prayer experience. In the book of Acts, prayer is mentioned twenty-eight times. The gospels focus on Jesus in prayer (twenty-six times in the four gospels, Jesus is found praying), or teaching on or talking about prayer (teaching: twenty-four times; talking about prayer: nine times).

In the book of Acts, corporate prayer scenes emerge. Thirteen times, the church is seen gathered for prayer, and on four additional occasions, a two-some or more is found praying. Private prayer doesn't go away, it is seen at least nine times. Again, we find this dialectic – corporate prayer and personal/private prayer. The book of Acts begins with the church gathered for prayer. Pentecost comes into a prayer meeting (Acts 2:1-4). Converts are urged to continue in prayer (2:42).

Acts – Let's review the book of Acts. In chapter one, we find the followers of Christ in a prayer meeting (1:14). The Holy Spirit, on the day of Pentecost, breaks in on a corporate prayer meeting, one that has lasted for at least a week. This is persistent, prevailing corporate prayer. It is prayer determined to receive an answer from heaven. It is prayer that refuses to go anywhere or do anything without the attendant power of God. In prayer, prior to the coming of the Spirit, the group considers a replacement for Judas (1:23-25); thus, leaders are chosen prayerfully, as was the model of Jesus. Those converted are invited into a prayer fellowship (2:41-43). When the Spirit comes, personally and corporately, they are compelled to mission. Then – thousands are converted.

In Acts 3:1, Peter and John go together to the temple at the hour of prayer for a corporate prayer meeting. The result is again – witness and mission. When resistance comes and persecution is raging, and, indeed, threats are intensifying, the answer is another prayer meeting (4:31). Imagine that! And when they had prayed, the place *"was shaken where they were assembled."* This is not merely the exotic, but a practical empowering given to *"spread the word of God with boldness."*

In Acts 6:4, when the number of disciples were multiplied and administrative duties tugged at the apostles, they recognized the need to prioritize prayer, *"We will give ourselves continually to prayer, and to the ministry of the word."* This is not merely a decision to persist in personal devotions, but a commitment to pray together as a leadership team – corporate prayer (6:3-5). Even the table waiters, the deacons, were chosen prayerfully, and then consecrated by public, corporate prayer (6:6).

In Samaria, they prayed corporately, as they had in Acts 2, and that resulted in the Samaritans being filled with the Holy Spirit (8:15). In Acts 12, the church gathered to pray for Peter who was in prison, facing a death sentence, and an angel set him free. In Acts 13, as the church prayed, the apostolic ministry of Barnabas and Saul was born. In Acts 16:13, a group of women gathered for corporate prayer each Sabbath, and those women became the seed-bed for a movement of God in the city of Ephesus.

Later, as Paul passed by Ephesus to reconnect with the elders, there is a poignant corporate prayer moment, *"And when he had thus spoken, he kneeled down, and prayed with them all"* (36-37). The Scripture says, *"They all wept!"* At Tyre, Paul stayed only seven days. Finding disciples there, they walked with him as he departed – whole families with wives and children accompanied him, and just outside the city, together, as a group, they *"kneeled down on the shore, and prayed"* (21:4-6). The early church prayed together.

Personal Prayer in Acts – Of course, Acts also contains moments of personal and intercessory prayer. Peter prayed (3:1; 10:9; 11:5), as did Paul (22:17). Simon, the sorcerer, asked Peter to pray for him, that he would not suffer judgment from the Lord (8:23-25). The Holy Spirit directed Ananias to Straight Street as an answer to the personal prayer of Paul (9:11). And there, Ananias prayed for Paul. In Acts 9:40, Peter knelt alone and prayed for Tabitha, and she opened her eyes and sat up – the girl came back to life, a resurrection.

In Acts 10, Cornelius was praying (10:2, 4, 30-31) and as a result, God directed Peter to minister to the Gentile and his household. The prayers of Cornelius were a memorial, a reminder before God, to which He responded (10:4). The private prayer of Cornelius is connected to the private prayer time of Peter, who was on the roof in another city, praying at noon (10:9; 11:4-6). We often see this triangle of prayer, by which God connects us to others through prayer.

In Acts 14:23, the apostolic leaders, Barnabas and Paul, prayed before selecting elders and commending them to the Lord. There we find prayer with fasting. When Paul and Silas were in jail at Philippi, their response was to unite in prayer (16:25). The result was a liberating earthquake, the conversion of the jailer, and an affirmation of God's hand on them. In Acts 22:17, Paul was in the temple in Jerusalem, and as he prayed, he was suddenly in a trance. In Acts 28:8, the father of Publius lay sick of a fever and was hemorrhaging. Paul *"entered in and prayed, and laid his hands on him, and healed him."* God was speaking mysteries. Obviously, personal prayer does not go away in the book of Acts.

Corporate Prayer in Acts – Yet, while personal intercessory prayer continued after the descent of the Spirit and the constitution of the Church, along with prayer for individuals – it is corporate prayer that leads. It sets the tone in Acts without leaving out glimpses into private prayer moments. When the church gathered, they prayed for a variety of things – decisions about leadership (1:24; 6:6; 14:23); for the Holy Spirit's manifestation (8:15); for repentance to manifest among sinners (8:24; 26:29); for healing (9:40; 28:8); for the work of missions (13:3); the release of Peter (12:5); for protection and safety (27:29). They gathered for prayer in times of crisis (7:59; 12:5, 12; 16:25); and to repent (8:22; 9:11). Even their goodbyes were moments of prayer (20:36; 21:5). They habitually prayed – the whole church gathered (2:42), and the apostles and leaders also gathered for prayer (1:14; 6:4; 13:3).

DISCOVERY MOMENT: Read a "Glimpse of Prayer in Acts."

Personal prayer and corporate prayer – the two need one another. You cannot sustain a personal, intimate relationship with the Lord in a group, and yet, because faith is never to be privatized, because He has loved us that we might love one another and has called us into fellowship with others, you cannot satisfy your obligation to God with a purely private prayer and devotional life. And conversely, you cannot satisfy your relationship with God on the back of public, at-church corporate prayer. At-home, daily, let-Jesus-be-Jesus-in-me praying is critical. This is personal prayer. Private prayer. Intimacy with God, through Christ, by the enabling Spirit, guided by the Scriptures. It is prayer that connects husbands and wives to God's throne – and creates the great triangle of love that secures the marriage and the family. It extends naturally into family prayer, family devotions, the family altar, church in the home. It engages the entire family, making prayer and the Presence of God something that is not strange and foreign to daily life.

At congregational prayer meetings, we catch prayer. We borrow prayer fire from others. We learn the language of prayer. We are mentored by praying with others, sometimes formally, sometimes informally. What we are praying about is important, but the fact that we are praying, and thereby learning to pray, is even more important. The paradigm shifts when our personal prayer times take on a spiritual life of their own. Sustained by daily time with God, we move from chronic and debilitating dependence on church-life to vital dependence on Christ-life by the indwelling Spirit. That does not mean independence.

In the early days, following our conversion, the church serves as a spiritual parent, guiding us toward maturity and dependence on God, the Father, in Christ, by the enabling Holy Spirit. The maturity of our prayer life and, as a consequence, a more vital spiritual life, does not constitute a break from the church. Indeed, it accelerates the connection. We now go to the prayer meeting with prayer-fire in our hearts. Corporate worship and prayer times continue to enrich us; we dare not privatize our relationship with God. We need the corporate experiences of prayer and worship. They stretch us. They move us into areas of prayer into which we might not venture alone. They expose us to the prayer burdens of others. Back and forth, personal prayer and corporate prayer. These are the two big wheels of prayer ministry. Out of these flow the other dimensions – mobilization of intercessors; prayer evangelism; prayer teaching/training; the leadership team; and the prayer room/center.

DISCOVERY MOMENT: Watch the video "The Two Critical Dimensions (At-Home and At-Church Praying).

Eighty percent of churches have plateaued or are in decline.[3] Ninety-five percent are congregations less than 100.[4] Churches plateau in the 15th year. Churches that are 35 years and older tend to have difficulty replacing the members they lose.[5]

One major USA denomination had 34,892 churches at the end of 2003. Of that number, 24,795 had fewer than 100 in weekly attendance — 71 percent of the total. Congregations with less than 500 in attendance numbered 15,770 — 45 percent of the total congregations. Seventeen percent had less than 35 attendees, and 13 percent, one in eight, were barely keeping their doors open with some 20 attendees.[6]

The typical church, of all denominations, has 75 in their worship service. We are a nation of small churches, many of whom are dying.

Two Sides of the Brain

The prayer effort moves forward on two legs – *learning* and *doing*. It also engages both sides of the brain. Teaching (left-brain) is not enough. Testing and experience (right-brain sensing, feeling, affect) is also necessary. The testing is in the doing. *Teach* (left-brain) and *do* (experience, which includes helping people past their fears of prayer, fear of praying aloud, of hearing and obeying the Spirit). Offer the *precept,* then *practice* it. And then graciously, gently, but bravely, teach into the learning gaps, and then repeat the doing.

Only 25 percent of the people who attend your church each Sunday are *Christ-centered,* spiritually vital people.[1] Another 23 percent feel, at times, *close* to Christ, but they have not crossed the threshold into the spiritual vitality that characterizes the Christ-centered group. There are two other groups that constitute half of your congregation. About 10 percent are exploring Christ, surprisingly they have not yet made a saving commitment to Christ. Another 37 percent consider themselves Christians, and they are growing in Christ, but are often 'stuck' and do not yet feel 'close' to Christ. Almost half of your congregation is either unsaved or feels somewhat distant from God. The difference between those in the other half, those who feel *close* to Christ, and those who are *Christ-centered,* is found in large part in their personal daily prayer practices.[2]

> Prayer tends to shrink to the boundaries of our own self-interests and preferences. And when it does, it dries up. God desires to expand us, stretch us and grow us, and that happens most profoundly in our prayer encounters with Him. To support a broad prayer effort, you need a means by which you can consistently, graciously expose believers to a world of prayer and needs beyond their comfort zone.

So many people attend church, hear songs about God, listen to talks about God, but never encounter God. The only prayers they pray are fleeting, 'God, help me!' crisis prayers. If you teach or preach about prayer, but you do not offer prayer experiences in which you practice those principles, your effort will fail. Teach on prayer walking, then prayer-walk. Teach on praying Scripture, and then practice it. Create prayer learning experiences: "Tuesday night, we will have a special prayer experience on praying Scripture." Do not expect all those who attend your teaching session to show up for the training experience. Our learning model is often passive, non-engaging and non-threatening. Doing is active, engaging and intimidating. At first, be happy with twenty percent or more in your prayer engagement effort. They will infect others. Teach and then practice. It is in the *obedience,* the application of the principle, that faith grows and that transformation takes place.

DISCOVERY MOMENT: Watch the video "Three Kinds of Churches."

The Three-Legged Stool

After years of considering these principles and working with thousands of pastors and prayer leaders, I have found these three, out of the seven markers of a praying church, are benchmark starting points:

1. A church-wide prayer meeting;
2. The development of a prayer leadership-learning team;
3. The encouragement of daily, personal prayer.

We are not casting aside the other markers of the praying church – mobilizing intercessors, prayer evangelism, on-going congregational teaching-training and the creation of a prayer room/center. In the attempt to simplify the process, we are, in the initial stages, synergizing three components of our effort – by intentionally training leaders, by congregational prayer engagement (learning by doing), and personal-family prayer. You are, in fact, mobilizing intercessors at the church-wide prayer meeting. And you should make prayer evangelism a regular, though not the dominant component, of that church-wide prayer gathering. In this scenario, the sanctuary, where the church-wide prayer meeting takes place, becomes the prayer room.

In the beginning, it is important that prayer training is primarily focused on the developing leader-learners. You might be tempted to offer this leader-training to the whole church. That would be a mistake. Your intent with this group is not merely training, but teaming. The important goal is to develop a prayer leadership team and allow the Holy Spirit an opportunity to create a bond of unity between them out of which develops a culture of prayer and humilty, worship and service in the congregation. You are training those who come to the congregational prayer meeting, incidentally, by 'doing' prayer. You are also mobilizing intercessors, since they are often the first responders to a call to pray, even though you are not yet treating them as a specialized component of your effort. While intercession and prayer evangelism are critical elements in your congregational prayer effort, don't make your prayer meeting an 'intercessory prayer meeting.' It must be bigger, broader than intercession. Intercession is a dimension in your prayer effort, but certainly not the whole. You want to balance your emphasis between transformational, congregational prayer and transactional praying.

I have seen pastors and prayer leaders create elaborate prayer rooms only to have them inadequately used. The members do not yet know 'why' they are important, nor yet, 'how' to use them or 'what' to either do or pray about once in the prayer room. They rationalize that they can pray at home as well as at a prayer room/center. They do not yet understand the power of corporate agreement in prayer, or prayer and place.

As you launch your church-wide prayer effort then identify developing leaders who will commit to personal, daily prayer, you will incidentally engage the additional 'markers'. For example, *you are training* the congregation to meet God by means of the church-wide prayer gathering – you learn to pray by praying. While that training is *incidental,* you are *intentionally* training a small group of developing leaders. You are also defining intercession, identifying intercessors, and directing intercession out of your church-wide prayer gathering – incidentally. You are keeping your prayer effort centered in worshipful, transformational praying out of which you do the transactional – petition and intercession. That re-centers prayer in healthier theology.

At some point, you will *intentionally* begin the task of identifying intercessors at-large, training and teaming, directing and debriefing. Intercessors do need to be acknowledged as valued contributors to the vision and mission of the church. Intercession is not a side-bar task completed by somewhat eccentric and overly-spiritual Christians.

Yet, for a season, concentrate on establishing your prayer meeting, growing leaders and encouraging daily, personal prayer – the essence of the *Praying Church Made Simple.* When you arrive at the point that the culture of the church is characterized by worshipful, transformational prayer and by crying out for the lost, so that prayer is creating both a new passion for Christ and a fervor about lostness with increasing evangelism activities by members, you are now approaching health! The prayer center, should you create one, would then be a valuable tool, a place at which intercessors might gather, the place prayer groups connect during the week to pray, in a church that is fully alive. The church is the only family that restricts new baby births to one day of the week. Normally, babies come any day and every day.

The Three Supporting Rungs
What binds your 3-Legged Stool together and keeps it from stagnating is:
1. On-going training and teaching
2. Mobilizing Intercessors
3. Prayer Evangelism

Let's review. The three legs are:

- The church-wide prayer meeting
- The development of prayer leaders
- The practice of personal, daily prayer.

These three legs are bound together by the rungs of the stool –

1. Training, incidental and intentional.
2. The development and the identification of intercessors and the movement of the entire church to become a missional intercessory community
3. Out of an intercessory culture, prayer evangelism bubbles forth, and from that evangelism activities flow naturally.

The crown of the legs and rungs is the seventh marker, the prayer room/center.

Look at the Idea in Reverse

The prayer center exists, at least in part, beyond the idea of mobilizing prayer and creating a visible intersection for the prayer effort, as a means to open the church seven days a week!

However, that is premature in a church that is not consistently praying fervently for the lost, not regularly engaged in prayer evangelism.

And that will not happen until intercessors are mobilized and the congregation sees itself as an intercessory community.

And that will happen only with on-going training and teaching.

3 FIRST STEPS

And that will happen only with leaders who understand the process, who are praying and seeking God daily, and calling the church to pray together regularly.

Thus, the seven markers of a praying church, the three-legged stool and its supporting rungs!

Building the Three Legged Stool

Seven markers, the four dimensions, the two big cogs, the three "praying church made simple" starting points, the three supporting rungs – sounds like new math! Anything but simple. This is a concept and, like a diamond, has many facets. It certainly is not a single dimensional approach to transforming the church into a house of prayer! It is complex, but it is the same diamond, the same house, the same construct, the same ideological matrix!

The Praying Church Made Simple is an attempt to help a pastor not be overwhelmed by the big picture and overall process! It is not an attempt to encourage a superficial approach, but to point out the primary arteries that get the blood and oxygen to the body. The three-legged stool of the prayer meeting (first step toward a praying church), developing leaders (leadership team), and daily personal prayer (first step toward recovery of prayer in the home); these three are vital, irreplaceable and the point of the greatest early leverage.

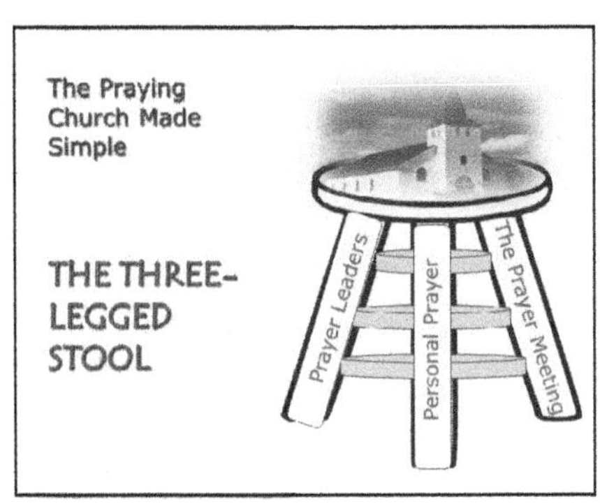

Your church-wide prayer meeting is a public commitment, a congregational appeal – "We must be a house of prayer for the nations." If you treat prayer as ancillary, as a support for your Sunday preaching service, like choir practice except, in this case, prayer practice for intercessors, it will fail. It must be seen as an essential. Yet, the appeal to participate must be grace-based, not guilt-driven. The ideal is weekly. Less than monthly, and you are not taking prayer seriously.

Milestone Two: Out of your church-wide prayer gathering, your prayer leadership team will emerge. Don't appoint prayer leaders who do not show up for this church-wide prayer meeting. This is a lead-by-example effort. Ask God to show you prayer leaders. Ask them to join you monthly, informally, in another venue, to consider how you might move the process forward. Let the group expand and contract. Gauge their faithfulness to the learning process. Develop a trusted relationship with them. That is critical for your own circle of prayer support as a pastoral leader. They must develop trusting relationships with one another. Watch them learn, learn together, learn from you and one another. Watch them grow in their own prayer life.

Milestone Three: Your goal is a praying people, a church full of believers who are vitally alive, and that means daily prayer over an open Bible. At the core will be a group of people with white-hot hearts. Don't move too quickly. Vet your prayer leadership team – learners first, then leaders; not leaders, then learners. Humility is critical to effective prayer, and no leader who is unwilling to learn can effectively serve the church.

By committing to the public prayer meeting and a monthly meeting with leaders, you and these leaders now have a greater motivation to develop a consistent daily time with God. If you attempt to nurture your developing leaders on the strength of your corporate prayer effort alone, you will fail. In, around and out of daily times of prayer, God will give you vision and strategy, prayer insights and guidance for both corporate prayer gatherings and for your developing leaders. You cannot lead a prayer effort without being a person of prayer. In a sense, this is the first of the three. And your prayer leaders cannot emerge as prayer leaders without cultivating a strong discipline of daily time with God.

Ready to begin? Call the church to prayer – have a regular church-wide prayer meeting. Do so not less than monthly. Weekly is preferable. Ask God to help you identify, out of that prayer meeting, teachable leaders, and begin to meet with them at least monthly. Then, daily, determine to meet with God.

DISCOVERY MOMENT: Watch the videos "The Praying Church Made Simple" and "First Year Steps."

---

1 Greg L. Hawkins and Cally Parkinson, *Move* (Zondervan, 2011), 90, 118.

2 Ibid, 181.

3 Quote by Tom Cheney and Terry Rials, *Nuts and Bolts of Church Revitalization* (Orlando, FL: Renovate Publishing Group, 2015), 1. See www.newchurchinitiatives.org/more_churches/index.htm.

4 Ibid, 12.

5 Ibid, 13. Quoted from "Churches Die with Dignity," (Christianity Today, January, 1991), Volume 36.

6 Royal Speidel, *Evangelism in the Small Membership Church* (Nashville, TN: Abingdon Press, 2007), xii.

GROUP TALK

1. Review the Ten Values of a Praying Church. After each of you has completed the rating sheet share your scores. Average them. Where are the areas in which you evidence the greatest need?
2. Review the Seven Markers of a Praying Church. After you have completed the rating sheet, discuss your scores together. Average them. Review the other rating tools in the Resource Guide. What areas need the most encouragement?
3. What are the "two big cogs" inside the Seven Markers? Why are they so important? Talk about it in your group.
4. Consider for a moment the personal prayer life of Jesus. Now, consider the role of prayer in the book of Acts. What can we learn from these profiles? What are your application points? First steps?
5. Identify the 'Four Dimensions' of prayer – make sure everyone can articulate them. Consider how they relate to one another. Did you notice they are two pairs? All related and yet distinct?
6. In the Seven Markers, beyond the Four Dimensions, are three critical supporting elements in the prayer effort. They are not merely ancillary or subordinate in value. Discuss these – prayer training, leadership development and the prayer center/room.
7. The starting place for *The Praying Church Made Simple* are the first three of the Seven Markers. Identify them. Discuss their relationship to each other and the whole effort.

ACTION STEPS

1. Review other rating sheets in *The Praying Church Resource Guide* available at www.alivepublications.org. At the very beginning of your experience, you may want to review all of the rating sheets and do the exercises as a matter of drill. You will then establish a benchmark of your current status and later your progress. See Resource Disc for additional Rating Sheets.
2. Consider the prayer life of Jesus. Review that section in the chapter.
3. Make sure everyone understands the 'four dimensions' of prayer ministry and how they relate together.
4. Differentiate the three simple starting points.

MILESTONE ONE

Things you should have in place now!

Launch a Church-Wide **PRAYER MEETING**

Prayer meetings abound in the book of Acts. The church itself was born out of a prayer meeting. Launch a weekly corporate prayer gathering or reinvigorate your Church-Wide Prayer Meeting.

Don't worry about numbers – at first. Have a prayer meeting if it is only you and God! Persist.

Remember, some folks will come out of guilt! Not until they come into grace-based praying will the stream of prayer clear up!

Some will come, responding to the old paradigm of prayer meetings – a 'request-driven' model. When they discover that the prayer focus is not about them or a needs-based approach, they may withdraw. And you may find yourself under fire.

Persist. Keep pursuing a worshipful corporate prayer gathering! Don't give up!

DISCOVERY MOMENT: Watch the video "Models for the Church-wide Prayer Meeting."

CHAPTER 2
Prayer Meeting Styles

If you simply start a prayer meeting on the ideological ruins of old prayer paradigms, you may fail. Think about your prayer gatherings on a broad continuum. Consider the 'content' of your gatherings, the style of leadership you will provide, and the degree to which and how the people will participate. There are four primary 'styles' of a prayer meeting. Each style prescribe different roles for the leader, and demands different content and varying levels of participation by the people. The continuum moves from low direction – in terms of leadership – to high direction. On the following chart, low or no direction is to the left; high direction is to the right. A higher level of prescribed content is to

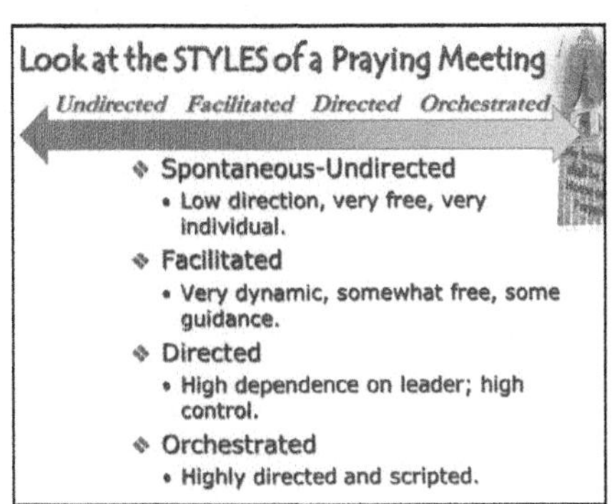
Look at the STYLES of a Praying Meeting
Undirected Facilitated Directed Orchestrated
Spontaneous-Undirected
• Low direction, very free, very individual.
Facilitated
• Very dynamic, somewhat free, some guidance.
Directed
• High dependence on leader; high control.
Orchestrated
• Highly directed and scripted.

the right, and that demands high direction. Low or no prescribed content is to the left, typically prescribing less direction. On the left, you will find the more spontaneous prayer gathering; and on the far right, a highly ordered prayer gathering is in view.

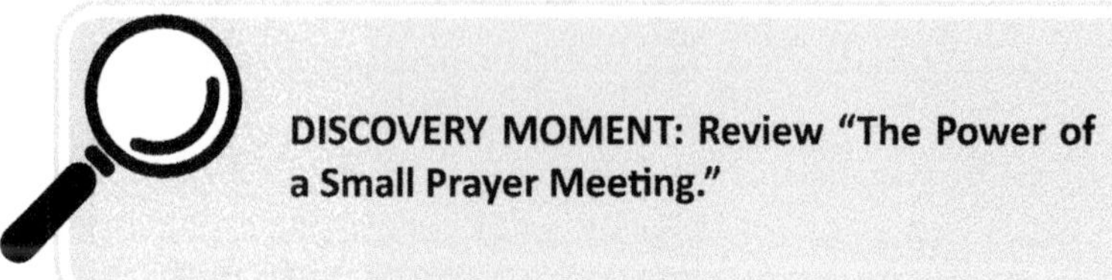

DISCOVERY MOMENT: Review "The Power of a Small Prayer Meeting."

Spontaneous Undirected Prayer

Pentecostal prayer meetings are typically in the far left column, as are some evangelical prayer gatherings. They are often undirected. Everyone comes in, finds a place and prays. Individuals are in the same room together but praying separately. The leader is passive in terms of offering direction and may not even be recognized as the prayer leader. Other than opening the meeting, if there is a formal opening, or dismissing the meeting, the leader is not a factor except for being an example in prayer. There is no planned content aside from the mention of a few individual needs or prayer requests. The focus is clearly on individual prayer. The praying is spontaneous.

This type of prayer event is natural for prayer veterans. With intercessors present, the gathering is often passionate. Such meetings can be quite emotional, tearful and expressive. A group dynamic sometimes occurs with everyone's passion rising and falling, like the ocean tide. Prayer themes, though unannounced, are sometimes noticed as the Spirit himself calls the church to the same page for prayer. In such prayer gatherings, it is not uncommon to see the mood of the entire group shift – from travail to joy, from heaviness to a sense of certain victory.

The Prayer Gathering

	Undirected	*Facilitated*	*Directed*	*Orchestrated*
The leader will need to be...	Passive Leader	Interactive Leader	Active leader	Directive Leader
Planning required...	No planning	Heart plans	Agenda items, ideas for prayer	Full prayer plan fixed, perhaps timed
Content ...	No Planned Content	Leader Discerns Themes	Planned Themes	Prescribed Content
The heart in prayer...	Heart determines content	Leader calls group attention to heartfelt content	Content is selected, but less important than passion/ heart	Content is prescribed and is intended to inform and inflame hearts for prayer
Focus...	The individual meets with God. Others are in the room.	Individual joins group meeting with God. Facilitated meeting.	Group meets God. Prayer is directed. Small groups/ individuals.	Group meets to pray with a plan/script. Meets with God over critical issues.
Collective Dynamic...	Individual	Individual/ Group	Group/ Individual	Group
Who gives direction...	Each <u>individual</u> prays separately. Self-directed.	<u>Facilitator</u> with individual/group prayer.	<u>Leader</u> with an agenda.	<u>Agenda</u> with a with a leader.
Behavioral Parameters...	Spontaneous	Stewarded Spontaneity	Spontaneous Moments	Controlled Spontaneity

Nothing can replace a spontaneous group moment with God! Nothing. That is the goal of spontaneous, undirected prayer. However, there are also dangers and downsides. One danger is a lack of boundaries. Tearful and heartfelt praying are poignant, and such praying is Biblical. However, emotion is not the goal. While intercessors and veteran pray-ers experience liberty in such settings, and excel in such an undirected atmosphere, others may struggle, feeling uncertain and even threatened by the open and undirected environment. They may also be distracted by the noise, the intensity and energy of everyone praying aloud at the same time. Further, in an open, but non-directed prayer gathering, some exuberant individuals feel a need to eliminate any silence – when times of silence and quiet are often are often the moments when the Holy Spirit speaks most profoundly.

An all-church prayer gathering and an intercessor's or intercessory prayer gathering are not the same. The all-church prayer gathering is not primarily an intercessory prayer gathering, though it will involve intercession. When your veteran and front-line intercessors gather for an intercessory prayer meeting, the style and focus will be significantly different. Intercessors spice up the church-wide prayer gathering, contributing to spontaneity and passion. They are essential, and yet, the church-wide prayer meeting is not primarily a gathering for those who consider themselves intercessors. It is for the whole church – beginning pray-ers and intercessory generals. That being said, one dares not attempt to control the Holy Spirit – that will doom genuine prayer. Neither do not want unbridled zeal or untethered emotion. You want balance. Spirit-energized prayer and emotional displays of forceful passion are not the same. There may be moments of forceful passion, but you must discern the difference on the prayer bandwidth between the emotional and the spiritual. Earnest emotion and authentic spirituality are often intertwined, but they are not the same.

Facilitated Prayer

In a facilitated prayer gathering, most common in evangelical settings, the leader gently directs the prayer process. He encourages the group prayer experience, but allows it to unwrap naturally. Individuals pray from their hearts, typically one at a time. The leader facilitates. His role is to connect the individuals praying in the same room, until a group prayer dynamic occurs. He encourages prayer – one person at a time. This may erupt into spontaneous corporate prayer – the whole group crying out to God – then returning to individual prayer. It is becoming increasingly common, especially in interdenominational gatherings, for prayer group leaders to urge everyone to pray aloud together, to use, as it is often called, 'the Korean method.' It gives everyone an opportunity to express themselves in prayer. And there is a certain energy that is so obvious when that happens freely and authentically. In facilitated prayer, after a few minutes of exuberate everybody-praying-all-at-once, the leader then brings the group back to a specific focus.

As individuals pray, the facilitator may note themes that surface. He may choose to point out those recurring themes, to call the group to 'camp out' around a theme and unite hearts over a given issue. He may, at times, refocus the prayers or transition to a new theme. He typically does not have a pre-planned script. He is attempting to follow the Spirit's lead in the moment. This prayer experience is highly dynamic. The leader, without the forethought of a scripted plan, may also introduce short scripts and prayer exercises.

Maintaining order in the context of spontaneity is a challenge. Such prayer gatherings are great opportunities to teach balance between corporate order and personal liberty, and they are a great context to teach discernment. Almost everyone in the room will recognize a 'take-over' spirit. That requires gentle discipline. A sincere, but immature Christian, may, in a moment of passionate prayer, also fail to recognize appropriate order. If a course of clear order is not charted, the young believer will not mature in corporate prayer, and the person who desires to exploit the liberty, will not only abuse the privilege, but will set a bad example. The challenges of such prayer gatherings can be indeed daunting, but the rewards are worth the headaches.

Facilitated prayer *moments* in a prayer service and a facilitated prayer *gathering* are different. You may, in the context of more structured prayer gatherings in your sanctuary, facilitate an unscripted group moment with God. When you do so, you are stewarding your sense of what God is doing in hearts. That moment may be the high water mark of the prayer meeting. It may last for a few minutes or for an extended time before you return to your script. You may choose to conduct a facilitated prayer gathering, a relational prayer gathering, without a formal script or a printed beginning or ending point. You will find that to be very different than having the sure footing of a prayer plan and from that plan stepping into a momentary spontaneous moment. Without a prayer plan, you are on the unpredictable ground of dynamic facilitation in a very free and relational prayer gathering. You have moved from dependence on a prayer plan to complete dependence on the Holy Spirit to grant greater liberty to the prayer-fire in the hearts of people.

This kind of gathering is best in an informal setting – not a sanctuary with fixed-row seating. By its architecture, the sanctuary structure, the physical form itself, is not designed for interactive prayer. It is platform focused with fixed seating. It is larger and more impersonal. By contrast, a relational prayer gathering is best, if it is limited, both in terms of the size of the room and the number of participants. Limiting the size of the room and number of participants assures that non-amplified, spontaneous personal prayers are heard by all, to maximize involvement. Too large a group and people are too intimidated to pray. They are reluctant to participate, and that defeats the purpose of the relational prayer experience itself. With too much distance in the room, hearing becomes an issue. Having individuals go to or pass around a microphone diminishes the spontaneity. An ideal size for a relational prayer experience is about 25-75. Remember *function* follows *form*.

Directed Prayer

A directed prayer gathering is less formal than the orchestrated prayer meeting, and more structured than the spontaneous/facilitated styles. Here, the leader is active, and there are planned themes, so this is not completely spontaneous praying. Nor, on the other hand, is it a tightly scripted and orchestrated prayer gathering. Individuals may be chosen to pray over or around designated themes. The content is planned for this directed prayer meeting. Typically, the group prays – individually, corporately, in small groups, at times quietly – and then, after a certain period of time, the leader guides the group to the next theme or planned movement of prayer. The prayer design for the evening may call for planned prayer moments and yet allow for spontaneous individual prayer, as well as spontaneous group prayer. In that case, the leader is directing the prayer experience and lacing in moments in which prayer is being facilitated.

Orchestrated Prayer

In the orchestrated prayer gathering, a script is used. It may cover material that is relevant to some immediate crisis or the prayer may be about a time-sensitive matter. It may take the form of prayer through and over a passage of Scripture that, if unfinished, will leave the experience incomplete. Such prayer gatherings need resolution. They need guidance so the group can pray to the finish of the passage or the agenda. Examples include: praying through the tabernacle, praying the elements of a solemn assembly, praying through a passage of Scripture, praying over the mission and purpose statement of the church, etc. In orchestrated prayer, there is less room for spontaneity. The content to be prayed, the script, dominates. This a good thing – especially if the script is Scripture.

In the directed prayer experience, mentioned previously, the content, though important, is like wood for prayer fire! There, whatever topics or prayer needs are not covered in one prayer session may be covered later. In the orchestrated prayer experience, the *content is* the important element, hopefully, not without fire. The purpose of orchestrated prayer is to touch the content, to raise the specific issues and connect them with prayer fire.

The orchestrated prayer meeting is at the other end of the prayer spectrum, from the undirected, spontanous. Leadership in this type of prayer gathering is critical. Individuals are not merely left to pray alone in the same room. There is an agenda for prayer that may take the form of a litany or a series of topics about which the group has met to pray. The prayer experience is planned. Even the content of the prayers themselves may be prescribed. Scriptures are planned to support the prayer process. They are read aloud. Appointed persons may be assigned to pray. In such moments, heartfelt prayer experiences need not be censored, nor should Spirit-led spontaneity. The main thing may not turn out to be the main thing. And yet, going into the orchestrated prayer experience, the leadership should have a clear sense that the prayer issues, the direction in prayer, even the planned participants and content, are those things that are on the heart of the Spirit.

Orchestrated prayer gatherings are helpful to stretch us out of our comfort zones, to force exposure to uncommon prayer concerns, to call people to the same page, to have them pray the same prayer about an important issue or concern. Orchestrated prayer experiences teach models for prayer. They impart language for personal prayer. They wake up burdens for continued prayer.

Biblical Considerations When Planning Your Prayer Meeting

1. *Focus on God,* singing and possibly by leading a processional (2 Chron. 5:1-13);
2. *Bless the people* at the appearance of God's glory, connecting the blessing to the Presence of God (2 Chron. 5:13-6:11);
3. *Pray* a prayer of dedication or consecration (2 Chron. 6:12-42);
4. *Lead the people in their response to God;* shepherd an appropriate reverent action (2 Chron. 7:1-4); here is the opportunity for a deliberate and intentional act that seeks to honor God and show Him reverence.
5. Bless the people and *attend the altar of sacrifice* (1 Kings 8:55-64).

To simplify, watch the movement:

1. The people focus on God.
2. He reveals Himself; His Presence is manifest and there is a blessing in His Presence.
3. Holy space has been created, the temple appropriately sanctified and dedicated. Preparation anticipates a meeting with God. In the Old Testament, it was a *place* that was consecrated; now it is a *people.*
4. The people respond. This is unscripted. The Spirit is now directing hearts.
5. There is a blessing followed by additional time at the altar.

So how do you lead a prayer meeting? Watch the movement again: Focus on God. Wait. When His Presence comes, leaders must create holy space and time for Him. At times, they must explain what is happening.[1]

Summary

The spontaneous and facilitated prayer gatherings work best in an informal setting with smaller groups. The more formal your prayer gathering, the more it begs for a structured environment, such as a sanctuary.

> Spiritual formation is the task of the church. Period... The church was formed to form.[2]

Prayer is connecting with God. Styles and modes of prayer vary – but prayer is prayer! Oneness with God is possible all along the continuum. No style of prayer is more spiritual than another, though all of us will find our comfort zone somewhere along the continuum of prayer. Pentecostals and some non-liturgical evangelicals may be uncomfortable in highly structured prayer settings. Those from liturgical churches may find themselves on uncomfortable ground in an unstructured and undirected prayer experience. Both forms are needed.

I recently found myself in a prayer meeting. A dear brother sat near me. As we prayed, over and over, he loudly repeated certain prayer words. With rapid-fire redundancy, he made *the sounds of prayer*. Tragically, he seemed to only be saying words repeatedly. We dare not make noise with holy words and call it prayer. Nor should we read and speak words from a book or prayer guide, without heart and passion, and call that prayer.

At times, I have found myself in a variety of settings – sometimes among high-church folk with prayer books. For them to pray beyond the form, to leave the structure of the safe and secure written prayers, produced a fear, an uncertainty that registered panic on their faces. I have also found myself in Pentecostal prayer services that needed focus, direction and guidance, when noise and emotion were confused with spirituality. We tend, depending on our backgrounds, to become entrapped in either forms or formless structures of prayer. In both, we miss the functional goal – a transforming encounter with God.

"Pray always," Paul admonished, *"With all prayer!"* (Eph. 6:18).

Do not be afraid to introduce new models for prayer. To offer language for prayer – the language of brokenness, lament, repentance, consecration, sanctification, renewal, evangelism and mission, all to God's glory. Discipleship demands discipline, and new disciplines are not easily conveyed. They stretch us. They make us uncomfortable. Eventually, they build and strengthen us.

In directed prayer, there is a script, but the style of prayer allows for improvisation. Traditionally, Pentecostals pray like jazz musicians play – no script, pure improvisation. One musician takes the lead and the others harmonize. The tune is made up as the music unwraps. An orchestra stays on script. Any variation is met with discipline – the individual instruments are lost in the sound of the whole effort. Rhythm, volume, intensity, the blending of the sectional sounds – strings, brass, percussion, reeds – all make a glorious, harmonic, singular sound. We should appreciate all the music of prayer – Pentecostal jazz and high-church orchestrated litanies. We may love one more than another, but we are to *"pray with all prayer."*

ACTION STEP: Complete the Rating Sheet: Seven Recommendations for a Good Prayer Meeting.

Death of a Prayer Meeting

There are a number of ways to kill a prayer meeting. We continue to make the deadly mistakes that sabotage healthy prayer gatherings. In our attempt to resurrect the prayer meeting, we sometimes reach for the childhood model we remember, without realizing that model may be flawed. It may not be a life-giving prayer meeting model.

1. **Informality as the culture**. Waiting until everyone arrives fails to see that the most important 'One' is already present – that's God! Honor Him. Start on time and, in doing so, make the prayer gathering about the vertical and not the horizontal, about God and not about us. Begin with two. God doesn't require a quorum. The waiting dishonors the

more disciplined saints and creates the time and space for chit-chat, which is so damaging to deeper encounters with God.

2. **Open microphone personal-prayer-request-praying** often assures that the prayer gathering will be narcissistic, self-interested, and all about God doing something 'for wonderful me.' Petition is a transactional form of prayer, and valid, but it is not the center of prayer. It is the *privilege* of prayer. Make prayer about God and then about His desires, not those we bring to the meeting! His desire is for communion with us; and His concern is for those who do not know Him. Emphasize communion with God and intercession for a lost world. connect the ideas of communion with God and personal transformation out of which we are godly representatives of His kingdom. too much of our prayer emphasis is invested in attention to our personal needs. Good prayer begins with God. It is worshipful at its center and at its edge missional. In between, God meets our needs! Make room for prayer requests, but don't allow them to dominate. Avoid open microphone prayer requests, but not open microphone praying. Have folks write down their prayer requests. In a smaller setting, encourage them to briefly *pray* their needs – not share them. Praying keeps you vertical. Sharing changes the dynamic!

> **Ten Deadly Mistakes**
> **(Ways to Kill a Prayer Meeting)**
> 1. Informality as the culture.
> 2. Open microphone prayer requests.
> 3. Unfiltered and indiscriminate information.
> 4. Talking more than praying.
> 5. Superficial 'bless' and 'be with' prayers.
> 6. Failing to steward the obligation of on-going prayers.
> 7. Assuming Spirit-led praying.
> 8. Forgetting worship.
> 9. Obligatory praying.
> 10. No continuity.

3. **Screen unfiltered and indiscriminate information**, ostensibly for more effective intercessory prayer. Prayer requests on behalf of others can end up resembling a sanctioned gossip session more than a heaven-earth prayer encounter. Teach discretion. Some things should not be shared in a

larger assembly. "As we conclude our prayer time tonight, we want to pray for others with needs, including those who are not here. As a matter of discretion, I want you to consider whether you have appropriate permission to share details of another person's struggles and needs, and what level of sharing might be appropriate without embarrassment to them." Our compelling need to share is often because we have not shared with God – not in a serious and deep manner. We then waste our tears appealing to others to do what only God can do. We ask others to do the praying we should be doing.

4. **Talking more than praying** is often associated with a 'prayer requests' model. In an informal prayer gathering, folks are prone to want to share. Sadly, the result is that the actual amount of time spent in prayer is diminished. In such moments encourage folks, "Pray it, don't share it. We can't help with the problem, but we can help with the praying. You pray, and we'll agree with you in prayer." Go vertical more than you go horizontal. We are forever commandeering others to do our praying. When passion and concern for another is connected to prayer, powerful moments occur. But when the passion is drained off in the giving of the prayer request, it is lost at the horizontal level. No one in the room is as passionate about the need as the one sharing it. Don't miss the moment by allowing the passion to be wrongly directed. Don't share it; pray it.

5. **Superficial 'bless' and 'be with' prayers** are just that – surface sounds we make out of habit. They lack depth. They are not connected to Biblical promise or power. They are wishes, not prayers. Good prayer goes deep – into God's word. "What does the Bible say about this?" It attempts to hear the voice of the Spirit, "What is the Spirit saying about this need, this moment, the person or family?" Such prayers begin to tap underground springs and invite heaven's fire. When a group of people discern God's will and ways in a

matter and begin to pray into that, the power of such a moment can be felt in the room.

6. **Failing to steward the obligation of ongoing prayer**. All of us have been in prayer gatherings in which a ton of prayer needs were unwrapped. We prayed the best we could. And then we left, and the prayer needs were forgotten. Most often, prayer breakthroughs come from prevailing, persistent prayer. That does not occur by the mention of a prayer need in one prayer gathering. We should sense the assignment of the Holy Spirit to carry needs, concerns and burdens. What provision do you make for helping folks discern their prayer assignment for the coming week or longer? Do you have a distributed list of needs that are mentioned in the prayer service? Is there a website to which people can go and adopt a need? Corporate prayer should push private prayer forward. That is, from the corporate prayer gathering, we should catch fresh prayer-fire and carry our share of prayer burdens.

7. **Assuming Spirit-led praying.** Evangelical and Pentecostal prayer leaders often implore everyone to "pray as the Spirit leads." This is an amazing assumption, that all present are directed by the Holy Spirit; that all discern correctly and are not only perceptive enough to hear, but empowered to obey. No one should assume such a thing. We are too often influenced by personal agendas, by the sights and sounds of the imploding world around us, driven by fears more than faith. We tend to want immediate gratification from God; it is a principle of the flesh-life. Simultaneously, we tend to avoid repentance and change. We seek God's hand more than His face, believing wrongly that His help is more in *our* prayers than *His* holy, transforming presence. A small slice of people, at most, in any prayer gathering are ready to be 'Spirit-led' in their praying. Most need someone who is led by the Spirit to direct the prayer time, and to collect the group into a spirit of and for prayer.

Death of the Prayer Meeting!

1. Is it a theology problem?
   The people don't see it as important.
   "We pray at home."
   "We pray enough on Sunday morning."
   "Prayer doesn't work for me."
   "Prayer is the pastor's job."
   SOLUTION: Teach into the knowledge gaps.
2. Is it a problem of style?
   "Do some people pray too loud?"
   Other object: "I am not used to that kind of praying."
   SOLUTION: Train on the importance of different styles and praying together.
3. Is it a lack of planning?
   SOLUTION: Plan your prayer meeting.
4. Is it a lack of prayer fire?
   CAUTION: Don't confuse emotion with spiritual passion.
   SOLUTION: Pray for the Holy Spirit to ignite hearts, starting with your own. Ground prayer in Scripture.
5. Is it too self-interested?
   SOLUTION: Push personal needs and prayer requests to the end. Begin with worship. Center in Christ. Pray Scripture.
6. Is it missional?
   PRINCIPLE: Good prayer is at its heart worship, and at its edge mission, and in between God meets our needs.
   SOLUTION: Make prayer for the lost, for nations, for Unreached People Groups a part of your prayer service.
7. Are their stories of answered prayer?
   SOLUTION: Tell stories of answered prayer. Borrow them. Build faith.
8. Are their corporate breakthrough moments?
   SOLUTION: When God moves and speaks – interpret the moment. Note God's presence, "Folks. God is here. He is speaking." Keep a record of such moments. Retell the 'word,' the moment in subsequent gatherings.
9. Is it a leadership problem?
   SOLUTION: Keep growing as a leader. Remember, effective prayer meetings don't occur because a leader shines, but because God shines. Keep the focus on Him.
10. Is the prayer meeting really a failure?
    SOLUTION: Pray for discernment. Is the resistance a struggle with the world, the flesh, or the devil? If so, press through. Is the Spirit being grieved? Obey God. Is there pride? Repent. Humble yourselves.

8. **Forgetting worship**. We run to God in petition – for daily bread (give us…), for disruptions and dissonance in our relationships (forgive us as we forgive…), for an escape from the problems in dealing with either evil or the Evil One, the world and its pressures and challenges (deliver us…). Isn't that taken from the model Jesus taught us? Yes – and no. It is a portion of the model, the petitionary portion. Habitually, we rush to pray our problems before we pray worshipfully. Good praying subordinates problems to praise. It *gives* God glory before it *grasps* at His promises. First, we pray, *"Our Father, who art in heaven. Hallowed be thy name. Thy Kingdom come, thy will be done."* Forgetting to hallow His name, to rejoice in the relationship itself, of God as Father, is a mistake. Prayer that begins with anything less than a focus on the holy and exalted God as Father is bound to fail. Worship is the first movement in prayer. Surrender is the second, "Thy Kingdom come." Alignment is the third, "Thy will be done." Seek God's face. Stand before a loving but holy God. Place yourself under submission to his Lordship. Join His kingdom. Bind your will to His will.

9. **Obliging prayer.** In an informal prayer gathering, prayer circles are common. And with them comes the moment in which someone prays. And then the person next to them prays – and from that point forward, everyone in the circle seems obligated to pray, taking their turn in order. It is a prayer killer. Prayer is best when it is free. Obligatory prayer, even out of courtesy, "It's my turn. I have to say – pray – something," is often shallow and contrived. Train people, inside each circle, to state clearly, "We are going to pray, but not everyone here has to pray. Let's have two or three express their prayers aloud, and then see what God might have us do next. I'll pray, and then anyone in the circle can respond in prayer." Free the circle.

10. **No continuity**. Prayer meetings are gatherings in which a group has entered heaven's courtroom and filed petitions – and those should be reviewed, not as a matter of rote,

but as a matter of the record of God encounters. Connect your prayer gatherings together. "Last time, we sensed God speaking to us about...We spent time praying in the Biblical passage of...God impressed several with the same idea... Tonight, I want you to open your Bibles to...We want to continue to pursue what God was doing last time."

DISCOVERY MOMENT: Review "Just a Prayer Meeting" and "Death of the Prayer Meeting."

The Bible is meant to be our prayer book. From it, we draw on God's promises. To it, we conform our thinking and acting. By it, we measure spiritual normalcy in a crazy world. It provides for us the character template of our Creator. It defines who we were meant to be. It gives us God's names. It details His acts in history. It provides a record of God in Christ, on the earth, behaving and speaking as a man. Out of the Bible, particularly, the psalms, we learn the language of praise and prayer. As we meditate on the Scripture and pray it, we find the words alive, full of life and energy. And that is because the Word itself is alive (Heb. 4:12). It is the sword that the Spirit animates (Eph. 6:17). Praying the Word of God gets us closer to the will of God faster than any other action. As a group prays Scripture together, it is drawn together in unity, aligned for action. Praying the language and concepts of the Bible lead us to begin to speak the language of the Bible, and to act on its concepts by faith. Hearing the Word engenders faith (Rom. 10:7), and that is true, especially as we hear ourselves pray Spirit-quickened Scripture.

Prayer Meeting Breakthroughs

1. **When holiness is championed.** When a prayer meeting encounters a holy God and spontaneous confession of sin takes

place, it is a breakthrough, and often the sign of the beginning of a revival. With concealed sin, prayer will always be hindered (Psa. 66:18; Jer. 31:34; 1 John 1:9). When holiness is championed, not only is sin more clearly revealed, but wholeness is in view as well. Holiness is a measure of health, vitality and godliness. It is our goal – to be like the Father.

2. **When the Word of God is prayed** with the anointing of the Spirit, faith rises – walls fall, healings result, rain comes, provision is evident (James 1:5-8).

3. **When folks obey God** – by sincerely and simply praying. Sometimes in symbolic action. Sometimes in repenting. Sometimes in posture – standing, kneeling, getting prostrate, breakthrough comes. "*He gives the Holy Spirit to those who obey Him*" (Acts 5:7). In the same same way, disobedience quenches the Spirit. It is a form of defiance, rebellion or stubbornness (1 John 3:21-23).

4. **When folks become real, transparent**, and without hypocrisy, breakthrough comes. The word hypocrite was used in the first century to denote the acting profession. Actors were hypocrites; that is, they pretended, at least on stage, to be someone other than themselves. When we lack integrity, genuineness in real life, we are acting – pretending, projecting an image. It is duplicitous. It is not transparent, and authenticity is what brings a breakthrough (James 5:16).

5. **Where brothers dwell together in unity**, God promises to sit up on the edge of His throne and command blessing in such a place. The problem is rarely the darkness or the condition of the world. Rather, we have not qualified for the blessing of God due to our disunity. Unity is not a nice, optional thing. Rather, it is the essence of Trinity – and to lack unity is to resemble the fragmented and competitive kingdom led by Lucifer more than the kingdom of God (Psa. 133).

6. **When reconciliation occurs.** When someone is so moved by the grace of God that they make their way across a room to another person and make amends, forgiving and asking for forgiveness, dry eyes are hard to find. Micro-reconciliations echo macro-reconciliation – across a whole congregation, sometimes

a whole city or nation. When the first movers of reconciliation act and unify, it triggers additional relationship adjustments up and down the continuum. Forgiveness sets off celebrations in heaven (Mt. 18:21-22; 6:14-15; Psa. 33:13; John 13:34). It is sometimes the determining factor in angelic activity.

7. **When the prayers are to please God.** Twice in James 4, as James describes 'praying amiss,' he mentions 'pleasure.' Self-interested praying, focused on us and our desires, constitutes the essence of praying amiss. The first goal of prayer is to please God. The great moment is when God says, *"This is my beloved in whom I am well pleased..."* (Mat. 3:17). We, too often, pray to get God to please us, at times for what we perceive to be noble kingdom causes. Praying with a narcissistic, pragmatic, self-interested outcome is always wrong praying. Wrong motives get us nowhere. But surrender – not only to the will of God, but to the ways of God and the timing of God – that crushes self. Examine your motives. Are you praying out of an affair with the world? (James 4:1-5).

8. **When strongholds are pulled down.** No believer wants to admit to the presence of personal and family idols. Around idols, the ideological strongholds of the Evil One form in our lives, our hearts and minds. Idols are 'his stuff' left in our house, and he claims, on the strength of its presence, a right, some level of power over us. The problem is not the image, per se, but the imaginations, the thought constructs around a particular unbiblical and ungodly idea. We are unconsciously influenced by idea patterns, thought matrixes that lack the imprimatur of a holy God. When we pull down these inner strongholds, raise in their place biblical ideas, a power shift occurs. Worship is freed. Bondage is broken. When an individual, a family, or even a whole church deals with crippling fear, and gets faith, for example, or the concept of God's blessing, or more importantly, perhaps, a sense of humility and awe before His holiness, it elevates corporate life. It changes actions and relating styles (2 Cor. 10:4; Ez. 14:3). It frees the church. It displaces the Evil One, breaking his power.

9. **When God comes.** You can't make God show up, even at a prayer meeting in His honor. Of course, God is always present –

but we long for the manifest Presence of God. Not every prayer meeting should be measured by some 'Wow!' factor. But we all need to be in prayer meetings that rattle us with the very real Presence of God. Such corporate moments are measurably impactful, when a 'God moment' is shared by all, and not merely an affect that happens to only one. In such moments, 'all' are filled. 'All' see the light! The world-shifting prayer meeting in Acts 2 was a once-for-all-time prayer meeting, yet it is a prototype for all our prayer gatherings. We wait to be filled with the Spirit so profoundly that we will be enabled to be a more effective witness. We long for a city-shaking move of God. And we know only God can do such a thing. What we must also know is that the disciples gave themselves to continuous prayer – for days! God comes as we tarry. As we gather for prayer – He comes into our midst. No gathering, no coming of God. No tarrying, no effective invasion of the Spirit, not only to us, but through us to shake a city (Acts 2; Isaiah 40).

10. **When people wonder.** We have lost our awe of God. God has been placed in the pantheon of other gods. People are no longer awestruck with His very real power and presence. In a prayer meeting where there is breakthrough wonder returns. Awe is evident, and with it reverence. A healthy fear of God emerges. Our faith must be more than a collage of moral imperatives, more than an idea, more than a religious philosophy. We serve a living, fire-breathing God. Tremble before Him. There will be little wonder about Jesus, about God the Father, until there is a new level of encounter with God in prayer that brings wonder and amazement. This is not a plea for petty theatrics – this is about exposure to God that puts all on their face. It rights respect for God in a skeptical and cynical culture. Pagans believe. Agnostics come to the cross. Atheists give up in surrender. Lives are reordered. God comes.

---

1 John Franklin, *And the Place Was Shaken,* 59.

2 Dallas Wiliard, quoted by James. C. Wilhoit, *Spiritual Formation as if the Church Mattered: Growing in Christ through Community* (Grand Rapids, MI: Baker Academic, 2008), 9.

GROUP TALK

1. There are *Four Styles of Corporate Prayer* mentioned here. They represent a continuum. Identify those styles and differentiate between them.
2. What is the most common style used at your church?
3. Which styles have you experienced? Which styles have not been experienced by members of your team?
4. Do each of you have a preference? Why? Is your preference merely the corporate style you have experienced most?
5. What would be 'stretching' for the people you lead?
6. What could become a breakthrough for you? For your congregation?
7. Plan a prayer service with all four elements.

CHAPTER 3
Relational Prayer Experiences

What kind of prayer meeting will you have? Ever heard the phrase *function* follows *form*? When God invited man to meet Him after the fall, it was near or over the shed blood of an innocent animal (Gen. 3:21). The context (form) created the climate for the redemptive moment (function). Cain and Abel met God at an altar (form), bringing gifts. Abel brought a blood sacrifice. His offering (function) was accepted, while that of Cain was rejected. Certainly, the acceptance of the sacrifice had to do with more than its form – animal or vegetable. It was an issue of the heart as well. Form informs and shapes function infusing it with reverence and appropriate respect for God. Abel had it; Cain did not. Abel observed the form; Cain did not.

Noah too offered blood sacrifices on an altar after emerging from the Ark (Gen. 8:20). Abraham seemed to build altars everywhere (Gen. 12:5-7, 8; 13:3-4, 17-18), among them, sacrificial blood altars. Ultimately, when Israel came rumbling out of Egypt, God stopped them at Sinai and gave them a tabernacle (Ex. 25:1-9), a kind of grid or model for approaching Him, a *form* to *inform,* to guide the experience of meeting with Him, the *function* of worship. The tabernacle had two altars – one for sacrifice and the other for communion and intercession. Function always follows form and form is informed by spiritual insight.

We have a protocol in the idea of an altar – a place, a sacred place, therefore, a consecrated holy space. At this altar, a daily morning and evening sacrifice was demanded. The Sabbath, the new moon, the festivals, all marked times to meet God (form). Thus, you have sacred space and sacred seasons. A place and time for meeting God regularly and systematically. Out of the *fixed form* emerges a *flexible principle.* We know we can pray anywhere and we should pray everywhere. And yet, if you do not pray regularly and systematically, thus sanctifying both time and place, prayer too often becomes shallow and superficial, sporadic and too casual. The informed form protects the principle and keeps it from being lost in flexibility. First law, then grace – that is the standard.

The altar, a form, a symbol of prayer, was a place of fire and of purification. There is always *fire* in prescribed, godly *forms.* They are intended to point to spirit and life. The power is not precisely in the form, but in the spiritual principle it symbolizes. The altar was also, in the ancient world, a place of light. It was a place of death, a bloody place, demanding the death of sin and trespass (Lev. 4-5), self-interest and division, and then inviting the consecration of self (Lev. 1; Rom. 12:1-2). The death of sin and self allowed the altar to become a place of reconciliation and forgiveness, and it still does. Then, in the peace/fellowship offering, the altar became a table, a place of feeding (Lev. 3). Prayer is bloody and agonizing. Prayer is insightful and light. Prayer is unifying and edifying. The form is intended to inform us.

The Institute for Natural Church Development (NCD) has data from 40,000 congregations in 70 nations on six continents. They have discovered that 31 percent of those attending small churches are actively using their gifts and talents to serve God, compared to 17 percent in mega churches. In addition, 46 percent of members in small churches are active in a small group compared to 12 percent in at the large membership church.[4]

In the Old Testament, tangible forms, like the altar and the sacrificial ceremony, are fraught with intangible ideas. Although we are free from the legal demands of these forms, the forms continue to inform us about the manner, the function, of approaching God. We need, for example, regular times and a place to gather to meet God.

The very structure, the physical form of a room itself, will determine, in part, the kind of prayer meeting you will have. The prayer meeting conducted in the sanctuary will be, because of the formal setting – the nature of the room – more *formal.*

Consider the setting. Remember, function follows form. Are you in a sanctuary? If so, the elements – the formal and fixed setting, the seating area arranged to focus on the stage – move you toward a directed leader-centered prayer encounter. Here participants are typically moved to be more passive.

Are you in a meeting area where the chairs can be moved about, placed in a circle or in concentric circles? Now, you have the capacity for a relational and very dynamic prayer encounter in which a facilitator may offer some guidance but participants are free to pray, to read scripture, to sing! This is highly dynamic, though not aimless or without focus.

If you use a room other than the sanctuary and arrange your chairs in rows, facing some focus area and a lecturn, you have retained the *form* of the sanctuary and constrained peer freedom (function) in the gathering. Home-based prayer gatherings, depending on the configuration of the meeting area (form), tend to be relational and informal, although they could arguably be structured.

Since prayer can take place anywhere, and each venue varies in terms of the potential group dynamic, the possibilities are incalculable – a campfire prayer gathering, street-corner prayer, an outside assembly on courthouse steps, gatherings around the flagpole on school campuses.

There are two primary variations. One moves between formal and informal. The other between a directed-orchestrated experience or one that is relational and spontaneous. You need both.

Formal Prayer Services

Components of a more formal gathering may include an invocation, song(s), greeting, then prayer and more prayer, with a formal benediction. Yet, the heart of any prayer gathering is real prayer. This is biblical prayer, whether it is prescribed (litany) or spontaneous (offered individually or corporately) within small groups or private times of silence and prayerful reflection. Laced into prayer moments, using either model, are songs, Scripture engagement, silence and praise. The nature of the prayers themselves may vary. They may be worshipful, declarative, repentant, prayers of consecration, prayers for the anointing and infilling of the Spirit, prayers that affirm Biblical concepts (the names of God, the character of God, the love of God, the holiness of God, the truth of God, or some Scriptural text).

Prayers of petition, prayer needs and requests, are appropriate but they must not be the center of a transformational prayer service. Equally important is intercession. Prayer from the office of the church, typically led by the pastor, is critical – for the mission of the church, the harvest and the missionary endeavor: the nation and its government at various levels; the community, and, of course, the lost. Intercessory prayer must not be the driving force of the prayer gathering. Remember, good prayer is, at its *heart,* worship and, at its *edge,* mission; and it's in the in-between where God meets our needs. The center must be worshipful, transformational prayer of both the individual and the congreation. Certainly, it is appropriate to pray for needs in your prayer service, but attention to needs should always be balanced. There should be in addition to personal prayer requests, an appropriate emphasis on the needs of those who labor for God far beyond our circle. The center is corporate transformational prayer – that is the greater need.

The benediction, in any prayer gathering, is never a mere closing prayer. It is a seal on the gathering. It is a means of beseeching God to act on the prayers of the people. It is a plea for blessing as we go in service. It is closure to the moment spent together before an open heaven. It can be a prayer, a song, or a litany – but its power is found more often in the declarative prayer of the presiding leader. Few benedictions are more moving than that of Numbers 6:24-26: "*The LORD bless you and keep you; The LORD make His face shine upon you, And be gracious to you; The LORD lift up His countenance upon you, And give you peace.*"

Relational Prayer Experiences

In a relational prayer gathering, the dynamic changes. There is still an invocation and greeting, perhaps some singing. Then the facilitator frames the purpose of the prayer gathering. Ground rules might be articulated. A focus might be suggested, a theme around which everyone prays. The facilitator may, at times, shift that focus, "Now, let's pray about…" There may be times in both the informal and formal gatherings in which the configurations of prayer are changed to triads or quads, or to partner praying. Typically, in an informal, relational prayer experience, the more who participate in praying, the more meaningful and engaging the experience becomes. The three dominant activities are: praying, typically one person at a time; the reading of Scripture without comment (the voice of God to all in the room); and singing, with the liberty for everyone to sing out as a song leader, acapella, with the voices alone harmonizing before God. At the conclusion of the gathering, the facilitator will bring the group to a benediction. He may offer a summary of what was experienced in the prayer gathering. Then a song, a passage of Scripture or a benediction is offered.

Components of the Relational Prayer Experience

There are three consistent activities in a relational prayer gathering.

Prayer

Everyone prays, typically one at a time. First, they are encouraged to pray bite-size prayers. Long-prayers tend to exclude – they dominate. They wander. They jump from subject to subject, as if the person praying, having prayed, has settled the matter. Bite-size, one-issue-at-a-time praying allows others to add their voice in a plea to God about some issue, and do so with both variation and agreement. It is a means by which a group can pray as one. One prays, and then another – about the same thing. As different voices pray around and about the same theme or issue wisdom often emerges. Consensus forms. Clarity comes forth. Balance is achieved. The problem and the solution is jointly owned.

It is also important that these typically should be first person prayers, at least in the beginning. "I," instead of "we." Not "I" out of a prideful posture, but of personal responsibility and disclosure. We should pray as ourselves. Pastors and leaders often use 'we' language when praying as intercessory representatives. That is certainly appropriate in some settings, but not to the exclusion of first-person prayers. 'We' repent is far less moving and impactful as 'I' repent. Leaders often hide in 'we' language. Make the prayers personal. No one person can pray for the whole group and simultaneously promote the idea of the priesthood of all believers. Everyone must repent for themselves. Allow the 'we' dimension to emerge as a matter of agreement after you have prayed through an issue, each person for themself. Third, the prayers should be sincere, forthright and earnest, believing the setting to be a safe place.

Scripture

Everyone is encouraged to have a Bible. Everyone is encouraged to read Scripture, providing the reference so others can quickly find the passage, and do so without comment. That is, pray without either preaching or pray-preaching. The reading of Scripture passages germane to the prayer subject at hand is a means of hearing from God. That should not be clouded by opinions. Comments and preachy moments, other than those by the leader for the purpose of setting up another movement in prayer, distract. They call attention away from the vertical to the horizontal. Encourage the reading of small sections of Scripture – no marathon reading, three to five verses is a comfortable length, eight-to-ten is the limit. Make sure the book, chapter, and verse is first noted by the reader. Encourage those present to read, then pray, without 'pray preaching.'

Our foundation and prayer book is the Bible, the Word of God; it is our authority. Prayers are both based upon and bound by the teaching and truths of Holy Scriptures. Encourage participants to launch prayers from Biblical texts. Have them choose texts that are brief (several verses, but usually not an entire chapter) and also on the point of what has just been prayed. This is not a time to inject a favorite Scripture or rehearse last Sunday's three-point sermon outline. The model is read the verses, then pray; pray the verses as they are read; prayerfully read and paraphrase them, owning the language of Scripture as prayer language. Allow the Holy Spirit to use your prayers as a springboard to encourage or enlighten others.

Singing

Everyone in the room in the relational prayer model is a song leader. The repertoire is wide open - hymns and choruses, scripture songs and gospel melodies.

Prayers are prayed, one after another. Then a scripture verse may be read. Perhaps two or three passages will be read, sometimes on the same theme, hopefully along the same idea – and when that happens, you know the Holy Spirit is calling everyone to the same page. Then, staying with that theme, another prayer might be prayed, and another, perhaps followed by a season of intense prayer. At times, the facilitator may need to say, "I don't think we are finished with the theme we found earlier in scripture, could we go back there and 'camp out' a bit in prayer?" After more prayer, a song may come forth or a song-fest, moments of sheer joy! All are then drawn into spontaneous worship.

This is a sampling of the relational prayer experience. It attempts to follow the direction of the Spirit in a context of worshipful prayer with a goal of personal transformation.

For the most part, in the relational prayer experience, participants sit and pray. Comfortable chairs are needed, especially for extended prayer times. Ask everyone to keep his/her chair 'in the circle!' This may be a battle, but physical withdrawal sends an unintended message of being disengaged, of being observers not participants, outside, even above the others, certainly detached in some way. Unity is symbolized by being an unbroken circle of peers, all in prayer, listening to and agreeing with the prayers of others. The goal is to hear God's voice together.

Spiritual formation is intentional, communal (requiring community), demanding engagement, possible only by grace through the empowering Holy Spirit, resulting in Christ-in-us, for the glory of God and the service to others in His kingdom.[5]

There may be times when it is appropriate to kneel. This begs for a carpeted room. Hard floors tend to create a colder relational environment. Carpet signals warmth. *Clean* carpet invites kneeling! There may be times when the group, even in an informal prayer experience, stand, often spontaneously in worship. There may be also times to draw away for a private moment of prayer, typically by instruction. Lying prostrate before the Lord is a more intense prayer posture. In reverent moments of holy awe, believers may go to their knees and then to their faces. Others may choose to move from their chairs and sit on the floor as a sign of humility! Still others, in seasons of intense group prayer, may walk about the room. Whatever the response, it is so important to not distract, to avoid drawing attention to yourself and away from the unity of the group and the work of the Spirit.

In a relational prayer experience, typical activities include:

- Reflective praying.
- Scripture reading, as noted earlier. The Bible is essential: each person should have a Bible.
- Periods of quiet.
- Private times for prayer.
- Small group prayer (six-to-eight: sometimes gender specific. At other times, allow mixed gender groups in the larger configurations, but never in the smaller settings of 3-5).
- Quads of one-another praying (gender specific, unless they are two married couples praying one for another. In such cases, three couples are better).
- Singing, as noted earlier, usually without accompaniment.

The smaller the group, the more difficult the spontaneous, unaccompanied singing becomes. With a larger group, freedom and the power of the voices alone is wonderful. Small groups and teens may need musical assistance.

- Another activity is the sharing of Scripture as 'a word' from the Lord (done without fanfare!).
- The high point is often communion – the group gathered around the table of the Lord!
- You may use a prayer chair in the center of the room, calling it the Father's lap or the Mercy Seat.

Quasi-typical activities are imaginary prayer walks! For example, you may say, "We are going to leave the room, and walk about the church campus, but I want you to imagine – by faith – that we are walking together in the city! As we walk, anyone can stop the group and say, 'We are now in front of city hall…or…at the corner of 1st and Main where the riots occurred last year…or …(any other place)', then lead in prayer for God's will in that place." You can, of course, stay in the same room – but the imaginary prayer walk allows us to get outside the room. It stretches us, making the exercise more memorable. It involves symbolic action, at the minimal level, walking and imagining. Remember, prayer knows no boundaries of space and place. I encourage the use of the language, "By faith, I am standing now at…(describe the place and proceed to pray for that place and the people who are there!)" Remember, prayer is quantum; it closes the distance between God and people; between our care and the need. Imaginary prayer walks encourage folks who have never prayer-walked before, to do so in a safer, less risky setting. They end up imagining themselves actually prayer walking the streets of the city or their neighborhood – and they talk themselves into doing what they had previously resisted, perhaps even feared. These can be powerful times of prayer.

At the end of some of these prayer sessions, I will often gather people around the communion table and encourage them, one at a time, to speak into each other's lives. "I want to thank God and you..." Now, they are looking directly at another person and calling them by name, and they proceed to say why they are thankful for that person! One after another, people speak "thanks" into one another's lives! Such powerful moments celebrate our need for one another and showcase unity. I might suggest, "Go to someone in the room now, and pray for the grace of God over their life and ministry. Do this one at a time." It is so powerful to listen to one person pouring out their heart for another, and to see the effect on the person receiving prayer.

The true leader of any prayer gathering must be the Holy Spirit! He guides all prayer. When prayer leaders perform or prayers are prayed for human ears – prayer meetings quickly die. The voice of God is heard most clearly from Holy Scriptures. Prayer services must involve our encounter with the Bible, its message, its call for repentance and its promises for revival. Allow the Scripture to be read! Read it and pray it. Singing is another way we express ourselves to God. Instrumental music can be the inspiration for prayer as well – as long as it is not the dominate feature. It must not replace prayer. And remember, musicians need to pray too. When prayer times are structured to always commandeer musicians to play and not pray, adjustments are needed. Environmental enhancements may include worship music, candles, dimmed lights, lighting effects, an enthroned Bible or cross, the table of the Lord, banners that offer varying prayer focus points.

A prayer service is not the goal – meeting God is the goal. Keep asking, "Did God show up?" And moreover, "Did the people meet God?" Jesus had one of the most incredible encounters of his life with the Father on the Mount of Transfiguration while the disciples slept. God may be encountered by some and not others. Keep asking,

"How can the whole assembly be engaged?" One way, even for those too shy to pray aloud, is by suggesting to all participants the power of symbolic action. Examples include a prayer procession, bowing before God, the lifting of hands as well as the laying on of hands. The latter has to do with the power of blessing. Consider the use of physical symbols: water, oil, bread, wine, etc.

DISCOVERY MOMENT: Read "Toward a Better Theology of Prayer."

Learning to Pray Together

Here are some great 'starter' ideas for teaching people to pray together. Mark Howell points out that a real challenge and a very common fear is that of public speaking. For some, it is their greatest fear. That is exacerbated by the idea of talking to God. Many folks think 'King James English' is essential for good praying – 'thee, thou' and the like! High-sounding phrases sprinkled with Bible verses, and good intercessory oomph![1]

Here are some ideas that Mark suggests, adapted here:

- Delineate a prayer focus. For example, "Tonight, we are going to pray for a deeper relationship with God. Nothing else." Or, "Our prayer focus tonight is on folks who do not have a relationship with God."

- Read a psalm and pray it. Or choose another passage of Scripture. Let the language of the Bible inform the prayers.

- Choose a Bible *prayer* passage, not merely a Bible passage, but a Bible-prayer. Have each participant open their Bible or have printed copies. Read and briefly comment on each verse or phrase. Then go vertical. Ask participants if they can 'pray it,' taking the conversational observations and praying them to God. At first, it might seem awkward, but only because we are more accustomed to talking to one another than to God. But watch how so much changes when the conversations go vertical.

- Encourage each person to choose a prayer passage and develop their own prayer.
- Put a chair in the center of the room and invite folks to the chair. Call it 'the Father's lap' or the 'Mercy Seat.' Have them mention one thing they desire from God. Or some burden they are carrying alone with which they need help. Have them *pray* it, not *say* it. Then allow others to pray with them and for them.
- Use word or phrase sentence completion prayers as ice breakers. For example, "God, I need your help with __________." "Lord, I'm so grateful for _______________." "Lord, you have been to me like _______________."
- Group the attendees in triplets for a time of prayer.
- Help folks get prepared. Pass out paper or index cards along with a pen. Make it easy and give each person time to write out a simple one sentence prayer need. They can choose to remain anonymous for this one. Swap cards. It is easier to read someone else's need, at least at times, than our own.
- On the back of the card, ask each person to list one thing for which they want to give gratitude to God. "Lord, I am so grateful for _______________."
- Designate a 'Jesus chair' in the middle of the room. *"Where two or three come together in my name, there am I with them"* (Mt. 18:20). Say, "Folks, imagine if Jesus was here in the room! Well, He is! Anyone want to talk with Him?" Arrange another chair opposite the empty chair. Then gather the crowd around. Allow one after another the privilege of 'talking to Jesus.' Then gather round and pray over them.

Additional Ideas for Church Prayer Activities

- **Conduct a Prayer Revival** – a week of nightly prayer meetings. Do a mix of sanctuary, directed prayer and informal, relational prayer.
- **Create a Prayer Chain.** It is an old-fashioned, telephone calling plan where one calls another who then calls another, until all have heard. It passes along urgent prayer needs quickly. More complete information can be posted on the prayer request section of the church website (if you have the capacity for quick posting).

ACTION STEP: Complete the Rating Sheet: Ten Indicators for a Healthy Prayer Theology

- **Create a Prayer Matrix.** It is a variation of a prayer chain, but with flexibility. In a matrix, you are connected to three others. One person calls you, and then you call another of the two connected to you. In a chain, if one person fails to call the next link – the chain fails. In a matrix, two failures are required. It is more relationally dynamic.
- **Encourage Members to Form Prayer Triads** – and meet for prayer monthly, if not weekly. These triads are focused on transformational prayer, not transactional prayer. The small, covenantal groupings allow for intimacy and confidentiality. They should be prayerful in nature. The heart of that prayer should be *to be like Jesus*. Once a year, ask each triad to invite a fourth member into their group to experience triad praying for 4-6 weeks. Then, have that person spin off and form their own triad. Be flexible. One of the original triad members might spin off, leaving the newest man to become a member of the existing triad. Or, the four might become two pairs, and each find a third member to form two revised triads. A triad may also allow a newly developing threesome to meet with them and then spin off to become

independent. The groups must reproduce or the movement of prayer stalls and dies. Reproduction forces the group to have an external, missional focus. They are to impart prayer! That should make the modeling of prayer a quality issue.

- **Form Prayer Cell Groups**. These are larger than the triads, typically 5-10 participants. They are not as intense as the triads. These informal prayer groups may meet around a prayer theme or cause. They may be joined together by some homogenous factor: couples groups, professionals, educators, singles, young brides, singled grandmothers, friends of Israel – or any other common denominator. They should not be by definition, 'share' groups; that is, 'share' groups have their place and value, and may have a prayer component, but 'share' groups are not 'prayer' groups. Prayer groups practice prayer. John Miller, in his book *Outgrowing the Ingrown Church*, says, "Prayer meetings constantly tend downward, to either intellectualistic Bible studies or anxiety-sharing sessions where religious arguments break out. Christian people and their leaders are ready to do almost anything except get down to praying with power and authority in the name of Christ."[2] Good prayer time always includes worship and simply loving God through the medium of prayers.

  Multiply these prayer teams. Large groups are less effective, since one of the purposes of these groups is to learn to pray. In smaller, more intimate groups, trust can develop and folks feel free to pray aloud.

DISCOVERY MOMENT: Read about Prayer Groups in *The Praying Church Resource Guide* available at www.alivepublications.org.

- **Conduct a Prayer Vigil.** A prayer vigil can be any length of time. Participants agree to pray about some cause or issue for some season – for 24 hours or for a month. A prayer vigil can be held at a location – almost as a lock-in for participants.

Or they may arrange a schedule in which each takes a turn, a *watch* from their homes. Use a conferencing or online option to connect them.

- **Encourage Senior Intercessors.** At a church in Michigan, senior intercessors each adopted a young person for a year of prayer. They prayed for them. Occasionally, they sent notes of encouragement to the young people. But they never identified themselves. Some of the youth learned that *someone* was praying for them – but they didn't know who it was! Annually, a dinner and sharing time is held, and the young people get to meet the seniors who were their secret prayer partners during the year. Kids would say, "It's nice to know someone cares!" Or, "It helped me through the year!" And, "It makes me feel special." And the adults? "This has created a special bond between me and this young person." In prayer, you always give your heart away. Another senior noted, "Prayer is more powerful than I realized!"[3]

- **Conduct a Prayer Conference-Call.** This is a prayer meeting over the phone – a group prayer meeting. You will have to teach a bit of phone etiquette, but more people can experience prayer across the city without leaving home. You will discover a core group willing to meet regularly on a prayer conference line.

- **Facebook** is a great way to connect members. A prayer need can be posted and in minutes, conveyed to all connected members. Prayer responses can be posted as well, as can guide updates.

---

1 Adapted from Mark Howell, www.markhowell.com.

2 C. John Miller, *Outgrowing the Ingrown Church* (Zondervan, 1986).

3 Vander Griend, *The Praying Church Source Book* (Faith Alive Christian Resources, 1997), 117.

4 Royal Speidel, *Evangelism in the Small Membership Church* (Nashville, TN: Abingdon Press, 2007), xiii.

5 James. C. Wilhoit, *Spiritual Formation as if the Church Mattered: Growing in Christ through Community* (Grand Rapids, MI: Baker Academic, 2008), 23.

GROUP TALK

1. Review the continuum and the differences between the prayer meeting styles. Which style of prayer meeting might work best for you?
2. Explore prayer opportunities near you. Participate in these initiatives. Visit a prayer gathering at another church – listen, observe, learn.
3. Find your congregation on the continuum. As you grow your prayer ministry, look for ways to expand the buffet of prayer across the continuum.
4. Review the ideas of 'learning to pray together.'
5. Review the additional ideas section. Pick one to implement.
6. Plan a prayer service. Remember, plans are the wood we bring to the prayer altar. When God sends the fire, everything may change. Prepare. Be flexible.
7. Caution: Keep your focus on learning and exploring different prayer models and styles. Experiment and choose what might be best in your situation.

CHAPTER 4
Warning: This Could Be Hazardous!

R. A. Torrey believed,

> Prayer often avails where everything else fails...By prayer the bitterest enemies of the Gospel have become its most valiant defenders, the greatest scoundrels – the truest sons of God and the vilest women – the purest saints! Oh, the power of prayer to reach down, down where hope itself seems vain, and lift men and women up, up into fellowship with and likeness to God! It is simply wonderful![1]

If that is true, why do we struggle so with prayer? Why are there so few at the prayer meeting? Why is prayer treated like a necessary but unpleasant thing? The chairman of a pastoral search committee presented a composite list of desirable attributes for their next pastor. The list, taken from a congregational survey, was exhaustive. It contained 85 desirable qualities and skills, habits and experiences. It included communication skills, management ability, a pleasant personality, the capacity for pastoral care and more, but nowhere on the list was a desire that the pastor be a man of prayer, a holy man of God.[2] Amazing. Prayer, as a valued pastoral activity, was not even on the radar screen of the modern church member, at least not as a conscious thing or as a first thought. It is usually an "Oh, yes! By all means." When a thing is so casually assumed, so vaguely noticed and taken for granted so consistently without anyone actually stewarding its cause, shepherding the effort, protecting the quality and quantity of the prayer effort, it either slowly dies or goes awry. Prayer needs to be intentionally modeled, nurtured, and consistently refocused. It needs an appropriate center – for balanced growth. It needs a champion – and that must be the pastor, the shepherd, called to 'watch' the flock.

The current focus is on *the pastor's work*. We pray to make the ministry effort go better, to preach better, to teach better, to see a bit of the supernatural sprinkled on the primary contribution that we are confident we can make, even without prayer. By prayer, we endeavor to add an edge to what we are doing, to improve on it just a bit. Such prayer is an insult to God. It reduces the Sovereign to a helper, it seeks to engage Him in a way that places Him in a subordinate role. In prayer, we blindly assume that we can commandeer God's help while failing to honor His Sovereignty and *His utter otherness*. We forever want a Savior without a Lord, salvation without discipleship.

Our *calling*, though we prize it, is not nearly as important as our *created purpose*. In fact, what we are *called to do* happens most effectively and most joyfully when it rises out of what we are *created to be*. We were created for relationship, made in the image of God, quickened to life by His breath, endowed with dominion and given the priviledge of walking with Him in the cool of the day. The *doing*, rose out of the *being*. Jesus asked Peter, after his denial, *"Peter, do you love me?"* That is the created purpose – it is the relational. And out of that emerges the call and commission to serve, *"Feed my sheep!"* (John

21:17). No flock is safe with a shepherd who loves the wool or the work of shepherding more than the Shepherd. It is our love for the Lord, the relationship, and by implication, prayer, that allows Him to trust us with the flock *for which He died.* Indeed, to trust us with His bride. It is wrong to love another man's wife, and while love for the church, the bride, at one level is acceptable, even essential, it is at another level inappropriate and out of balance. A pastor's love for the work – indeed, even for the sheep – can never be greater than his love for the Lord. If we come to love the work more than the Lord, we are in trouble, and the church is then in dreadful danger. Our mission is not to cultivate a relationship with the bride, but to work to strengthen the relationship of the bride to Christ – anything less is dishonorable. We are *called* to 'feed the sheep,' but we were *created* to 'love the Lord,' and the first is impossible without the second. E. M. Bounds noted, "It is better to let the work go by default than to let the praying go by neglect. Whatever affects the intensity of our praying affects the value of our work."[3]

In the days and weeks before the tabernacle was set up after Israel's emancipation from Egypt, Moses raised up a temporary tent of meeting on the edge of the wilderness camp. It was open to all who wanted to inquire of the Lord. Moses would go into the tent, and the Bible says that the glory of the Lord came down on the tent, and the people would witness this strange manifestation. When they did, they would stand and worship. Inside, Moses had personal encounters with God in those early days after leaving Egypt. What happens when a congregation sees their pastor pray? Sees his lifestyle of prayer? Observes his routine of regularly seeking the direction and favor of God? What difference does it make that they see the cloud of God's glory and sense that the enterprise in which they are involved is no natural thing? That it is fraught with God's glorious Presence and it has about it a supernatural quality?

The Tent of Meeting – the Church Prayer Room

Every church needs a 'tent of meeting' – a prayer room, a prayer center, an ongoing prayer meeting! And they need to see a pastor who meets with God. They need to sense that they are not alone in the journey, that they have supernatural companionship for the mission. A congregation that sees a pastor deeply dependent on God, one that has encounters with God traceable to his prayer life, is elevated to another level. Without a clear conviction that the pastor is a holy man of God and evidence that he is attempting to lead the congregation in following God's script, there is little ground to inspire confidence that the church is the dynamic organism pictured in the New Testament. There is an interesting note about this, that is sometimes overlooked. As Moses met God, Joshua, the son of Nun, his young aide, accompanied him to the tent. When Moses left the tent of meeting, Joshua stayed (Ex. 33:7-11). He lingered in the Presence. And he became the successor to Moses. You will always find your future leaders in your prayer meeting. Those who do not attend are often the ones who are inclined to lean on their own wisdom and ability.

One of the underlying dynamics in apostasy is the trend that changes *"the glory of the incorruptible God into an image made like corruptible man"* (Rom. 1:22-23). The difference is worlds apart – the glory of God or the image of man, the incorruptible and the corruptible. The otherworldly needs to dominate our worship. When the focus shifts from God to man, from the other world to our own, Paul warned that the word of the wise is trumped by that of fools. Time and time again, Israel incorporated some aspect of contemporary idolatry into its worship, often with an edge of sensuality. Idolatry and sensuality pollute contemporary worship as well, perhaps, for the same reason – to appeal to a larger, wider spectrum of people – but such adaptations are always deadly. Today, we feel that we must 'spice up' worship to make it appealing. The result is almost always worship as entertainment and less time for serious, prayerful, heart-searching encounters with God. We are like the generation to whom Malachi appealed, the last generation before the silence between the Testaments. For that generation, worship had become tedious and uninteresting. "Oh, what a weariness!" they said of the altar. They sneered at God's prescriptions. They compromised the standards of participation (Mal. 1:13).

> Dallas Willard argues, "...Christian churches have been distracted from the central task of teaching their people how to live the spiritual life in a way that brings them progressively to enjoy the character of Christ as their own."[9] Willard charges the church with "a sense of spiritual shallowness and emptiness..."[10] To restore the church to its original purpose, and not an institution primarily focused on personal satisfaction, we need a "culture of formation."[11] Willard makes a stunning declaration, "I know of no current denomination or local congregation that has a concrete plan and practice for teaching people to do 'all things whatsoever I have commanded you."[12]

Battling the Spirit of Entertainment

In *The Church Awakening*, Charles Swindoll says, "Our world has lost its way. So it's no surprise when the church takes its cues from the world, the church begins to go astray as well. But must we resort to gimmicks for people to come to church?...Must we dumb down historic Christianity into shallow entertainment in order to pamper consumers? May it never be!" He continues, "I am convinced that the church doesn't need marketing devices, worldly strategies, live entertainment, or a corporate mentality to be contagious. Not if the glory of God is the goal. Not if the growth of God's people is in view."[4] There are fewer men who spoke out so boldly against the church as entertainment than A.W. Tozer:

> For centuries the Church stood solidly against every form of worldly entertainment...But of late she has become tired of the abuse and has

> given over the struggle. She appears to have decided that if she cannot conquer the great god Entertainment she may as well join forces with him and make what use she can of his powers. So today we have the astonishing spectacle of millions of dollars being poured into the unholy job of providing earthly entertainment for the so-called sons of heaven. Religious entertainment is in many places rapidly crowding out the serious things of God. Many churches these days have become little more than poor theaters where fifth-rate "producers" peddle their shoddy wares with the full approval of evangelical leaders who can even quote a holy text in defense of their delinquency. And hardly a man dares raise his voice against it.[5]

There is little time given to prayer in the modern worship event; it has become a production. Music and worship are not the same. A pastoral talk or Bible lesson is not the same as preaching. The 'one another' dynamic is being lost in large crowds, and authentic fellowship and discipleship are now endangered. The church lives from one big-bang event to the next. John MacArthur calls this "show time religion."[6] Prayer is not offered; it is not appealing. Fasting is abandoned, and when it is mentioned, it is always in one of its 'lighter' forms. Evangelism that calls for sinners to repent, for contrition over sin, has been deemed offensive language. The new evangelism is essentially turning over a new leaf on par with a New Year's resolution, the difference being the minor addition of God into the equation.

When we speak of the church becoming a house of prayer, we are really talking about a reformation of the church. We mean the difficult journey of producing a people who are vitally alive in God, who have refused to remain at the edge of faith, and have pressed by grace toward the center. We mean a church that is Spirit-led, where the pastor meets with God and the glory comes, and yet, one that is not marked as eccentric, that does not champion the wild and weird. Prayer is not optional. As Luther reminds us, "A Christian is no Christian if he does not pray." And a church is no church if it is not marked by and bathed in prayer. Salvation is a relationship, and the essence of any relationship is communication, or communion.

Someone noted, "If prayers can make a difference – save the

nation or the world, why have they not done so? Because, the wise man said, we needed a river of prayer, not a trickle."[7] Precisely. We are dipping our toes into the edge of the river of prayer and expecting miraculous results. We need to take the plunge and become 'a house *of* prayer,' and not merely a 'church *that* prays.'

The Four Dimensions

There are four dimensions to a praying church. By dimensions, we mean spheres of prayer, worlds of prayer, which need to be intentionally developed. Each is a distinct and entire realm of prayer.

The Home and Prayer

The practice of personal daily prayer and family devotions is historically, abysmally low. Only about four percent of Christian families have any form of family prayer time apart from a blessing at meal time.[8] We fail at our church prayer effort because of our failure at home. Yet, to suggest that a family is not a Christian family if the practice is being neglected is met with howls of 'works, not grace,' and a kind of horrified shock at the suggestion. In the mid-1800s, every Christian family was expected to conduct family worship. Failure to do so resulted in church discipline! Ouch. This tells us how far our faith has digressed in a century and a half.

Prayer cannot be foreign to daily life or the home. You will never have a vibrant, praying church until you have praying homes – that means praying people. But prayer in the home is not a simple matter. It is multi-layered. It is personal prayer, couples in prayer, and the family gathered in prayer. It includes formal times, but its most powerful moments are incidental. It is the power that is tapped, and the liberty that is demonstrated, when a couple spontaneously seeks God together. It is dynamic – the father and mother praying together, the son and father, the mother and daughter. The Old Testament prescribed faith celebrations for the home – Passover, Unleavened

Bread, First Fruits, Pentecost, Atonement, Feast of Trumpets, and the Feast of Tabernacles. The celebrations retold, annually, the story of redemption. They reinforced basic theological ideas – redemption, sanctification, giving, the law and the Spirit's importance, repentance, the harvest, life as a journey – a pilgrimage, and finally, eschatological consumation.

Most Christians have no similar home-based faith observances. It is not the presence of the synagogue that has made the Jewish faith so indestructible, it is the home observances tied to daily life. By these observances, the family annually and systematically revisited the stories of God's work in their lives – sin and bondage, the blood of the lamb on the doorposts, deliverance from Egypt and liberation from slavery, dependence on God, the tablets and the tabernacle, the harvest and coming kingdom. Christians have nothing that compares to such celebrations or even to the weekly family Sabbath gathering.

Many Christian families are developing a Biblical calendar for faith celebrations at home. Family prayer should also involve the recovery of the rites of passage that mark the spiritual development and growth of our children. Every family should be missional. First, by praying beyond their own needs – that means prayer for the lost, for unreached peoples. And if possible, by becoming a sending family. Family mission trips mark families forever. The recovery of prayer in the home is far beyond a simple daily Scripture and prayer, although that is a good beginning.

The Church and Prayer

In the same way, that the home is anchored by prayer, the church is anchored in church-wide prayer meeting! Not a gathering of intercessors, but the church gathered in prayer – for communion with God, to offer petitions, to intercede, and to offer thanksgiving. Out of a vibrant congregational prayer meeting should come the launch of healthy prayer groups. Then, embedded prayer teams should support the various endeavors of the church. Every ministry in the church should have a prayer team. The goal is the creation of a culture of dependence on God. That will entail a diverse menu of prayer for the church and throughout the church. At this point, you are laying the foundation for that expansion.

ACTION STEP: Complete the Rating Sheet: Prayer Ministry Survey 1.

Identified Intercessors

The organization of the intercessory ministry involves the identification of intercessors, in the same way you would identify volunteers, workers, singers, givers or any other group in the church. Intercessors should be taught. Don't assume that intercession is so native, so instinctive, that no teaching or training is necessary. This group desperately needs teaching and training. You will be asking them to stand between the church and the Evil One, putting them at greater risk than almost any other group in your congregation. Some intercessors function like scouts, who go ahead into potentially dangerous and unchartered territory. They do this by and in intercessory prayer. They need to be teamed for protection and confirmation. "This is what we want you to pray about..." Their insights and prayer nudges certainly need confirmation, but they must be taken seriously. Leaders lead, but seers (intercessors,

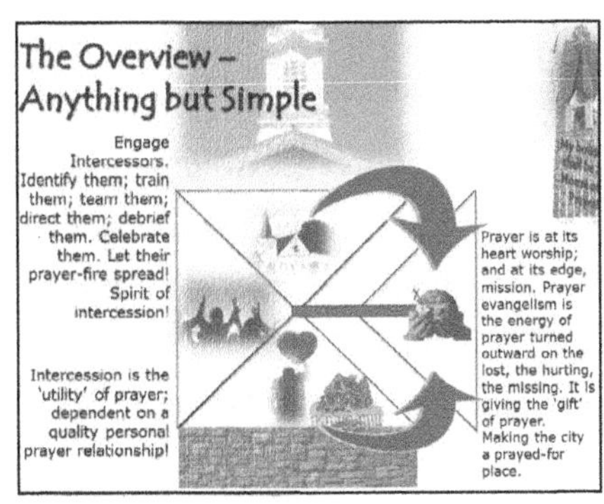

watchers) see. A system should be developed to share needs and steward the prayer energy of the intercessors, and a system should be developed to harvest the special insights of intercessors. A watch needs to be considered.

Prayer Evangelism

The prayer endeavor must have an external focus. The energy of prayer cannot be commandeered and spent entirely on the members or the efforts of the church. It must engage the unsaved, the unreached, the neighbors around the church and the city beyond it, the nation and the nations. This is prayer evangelism. We must give prayer away generously. The following are the four dimensions of prayer – spheres of prayer that need to be cultivated for the prayer ministry to be matured.

Building the Three Legged Stool

The two big cogs, at-home and at-church prayer, plus leadership, are the three "praying church made simple" starting points. They are the first three of the seven markers of a praying church, inside of which are the four dimensions. Sounds like a new kind of math and anything but simple. This is a concept, and like a diamond, it has many facets. It certainly is not a one-dimensional approach to transforming the church into a house of prayer! It is complex, but each facet is a part of the same diamond, the same house, the same construct, the same ideological matrix!

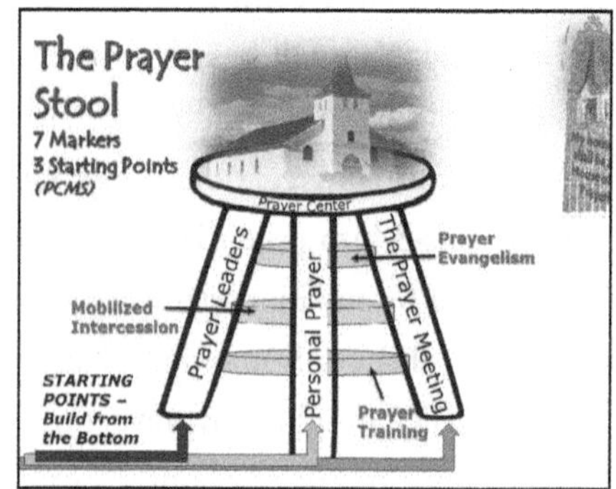

For a church to have all seven markers and develop

the four dimensions, you need a prayer leadership team. You need ongoing training and teaching that introduces all the various aspects of prayer. Finally, you will be helped greatly if you have a prayer room or center, a prayer office or counter – some visible connecting point that keeps prayer before the people and offers opportunities for them to be engaged in the growing prayer ministry of the church. Altogether, the four dimensions – praying homes, a praying church, identified intercessors, prayer evangelism – along with prayer leaders, ongoing training, and a prayer touch-point (room, center, wall, sign-up counter) – constitute the 'Seven Markers of a Praying Church.'

The Praying Church Made Simple is not an attempt to dumb down this big picture process or encourage a superficial approach, but to point out the primary arteries that get the blood and oxygen to the body. Here we will talk about the three-legged stool of the prayer meeting (the first step toward a praying church), developing leaders (leadership team), and daily personal prayer (the first step toward recovery of prayer in the home). These three are vital, irreplaceable and the point of the greatest early leverage.

ACTION STEP: Complete the Rating Sheet: Prayer Ministry Survey 2.

Yogi Berra, famed New York Yankee, once said, "When you come to a fork in the road, take it." You are now at a fork in the road. Take it. And get ready for additional Berra moments: "I made a wrong mistake," he once said. So will you. Probably a ton of them. But each of them will reveal an attempt to be dependent on God. Stay at the process. Don't give up. Those who drive in other countries often discover roads with no lines for lanes, and when they do exist, they appear to only be treated as suggestions. This is true with growing a praying church. There are few definitive lines. And when they show up, as they do in this book, they are only suggestions. You have to discern what God is saying. One man who was involved in an accident in a foreign third-world nation was asked by a policemen. "Why didn't you give the other driver his half of the road?" "I tried," the American said, "but I couldn't figure out which half he wanted!" God will show you what He wants.

You may have heard about the senior citizen who called her doctor and asked for clarification. "Did you say I would be on this new medicine for the rest of my life?" "Yes," the doctor said in a matter-of-fact manner. There was silence. "Well," the woman continued, "I was wondering if there was something else you needed to tell me… just how serious is my condition? Because, doctor, this medicine is marked 'no refills.'" Don't worry. There are plenty of refills. We are on a journey no one has taken before. This is not a matter of attempting to restore prayer to its 1950s norm. God is calling His church to a whole new existence, to be a house of prayer for the nations! This is new. This is unseen. We have not passed this way before!

---

1 R. A. Torrey, *How to Pray* (Moody).

2 Daniel Henderson, *Fresh Encounters* (Colorado Springs, CO: NavPress, 2004), 55.

3 E.M. Bounds, *The Complete Works of E.M. Bounds* (Simon and Schuster, 2013).

4 Charles Swindoll, *The Church Awakening* (FaithWords, 2010).

5 A. W. Tozer, *The Root of the Righteous* (Camp Hill, PA: Wing Spread Publishers, 1955, 1986).

6 John MacArthur, *Ashamed of the Gospel: When the Church Becomes Like the World* (Wheaton, IL: Crossway Books, 1993, 2010), 83.

7 Frank C. Laubach, *Prayer: the Mightiest Force in the World* (New York: Fleming H. Revell, 1946), 15.

8 Dr. David Stoop, in a website article, "The Couple that Prays Together" August 6, 2012, The National Association of Marriage Enhancement: Phoenix, Arizona, reported that when couples prayed together on a daily basis, less than 1% of those couples ended up getting a divorce. The numbers were one out of 1,156. Now, there is this new study that goes even further, a fascinating research project led by Christopher Ellison at the University of Texas, San Antonio, reported in the *Journal of Marriage and Family*. They looked at four

things: 1. The effect of a couple belonging to the same denomination; 2. Their attending religious services together; 3. Shared beliefs and values; and 4. What they did at home in the way of worship activities. The study looked at 1,387 couples. Those couples who shared the same faith, and who regularly attended church services together, reported a higher level of marital satisfaction. Second, couples involved in activities at the church reported an even higher level of marital satisfaction. The most interesting finding – when couples shared religious practices at home (Bible reading together and praying), the level of marital satisfaction was significantly higher. Those shared behaviors had a strong impact on marital satisfaction, so strong that the researchers believe that those behaviors could be seen as predictors of a strong marriage and, obviously, higher marital satisfaction.

Unfortunately, not very many Christian couples read the Bible together or pray together. The estimate is about 4% of Christian couples pray together daily. Pastoral couples who pray together daily are only about 6%. The important takeaway is that if you want to strengthen your marriage–and even 'divorce-proof' your marriage–develop a consistent pattern of reading the Bible together and praying together in your home. See: drstoop.com/the-couple-that-prays-together.

9 Dallas Willard, quoted by James. C. Wilhoit, *Spiritual Formation as if the Church Mattered: Growing in Christ through Community* (Grand Rapids, MI: Baker Academic, 2008), 9.

10 Ibid.

11 Wilhoit, ibid.

12 Willard, quoted by Wilhoit.

GROUP TALK

1. Why do you think the modern church has grown so prayerless?
2. Focus on the difference between our calling and our created purpose. Do you see the implications of the distinctive?
3. Is Joshua's successor role related to his potential, his native leadership, and military gifts? Or is it related to his lingering in the Presence of God?
4. Few congregations practice church discipline today. What would the response be in your congregation if conducting family devotions was a requirement for membership? Consider the gap between what was thought to be normal a few centuries ago and today.
5. Review the Seven Markers, the Four Dimensions, and the three beginning points that constitute *The Praying Church Made Simple.*
6. Talk about the big picture and the immediate task at hand, *The Praying Church Made Simple.* Do you have a grasp of the Seven Markers, the Four Dimensions, the Two Big COGS, and the Three Starting Places?

DEVELOP LEADERS

Learning Team Curriculum Options

As you begin to meet and develop leaders, you need curriculum for prayer training. Here are a few options:

The Praying Church Resource Guide

The Prayer Trainer's Manual

Transforming Your Church into a House of Prayer – Revised Edition (book and DVD)

Prayer – The Heart of It All (Book, study guide and resource kit)

The Praying Church Handbook – Volumes I-IV

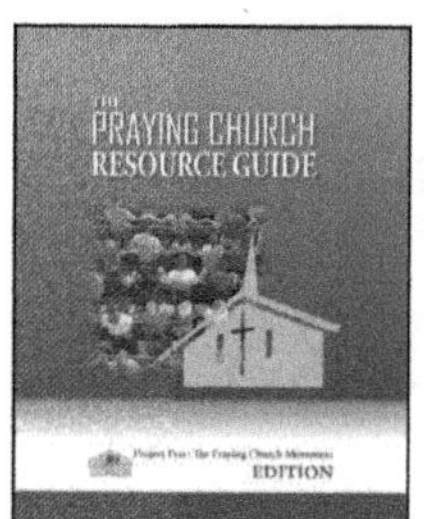

Available at www.alivepublications.org or 855-842-5483

CHAPTER 5
Developing Prayer Leaders

Thomas Hooker, a prominent Puritan colonial leader, called the Father of Connecticut, declared, "Prayer is my chief work, and it is the means by which I carry on the rest…" Harold Lindsell, author and longtime editor of *Christianity Today*, said it more bluntly, "Prayerlessness is sin." E. M. Bounds once said, "Those who know God best are the richest and most powerful in prayer…"

Bounds believed that "little acquaintance with God" was always accompanied by "a strangeness and coldness," which rendered "prayer a rare and feeble thing" in the lives of such people. And of course, that truncated their work in His behalf, not to mention their joy in the work.

The second leg of our three-legged stool is *developing leaders – praying leaders*. In step one, you started a prayer meeting or some type of church-wide, regular prayer engagement – the first leg of the stool. And you watched who showed up, perhaps with some surprise.

You are now looking for potential prayer leaders. There may be exceptions, but, generally, you want prayer leaders who show up for prayer meetings. It is not those who *say* prayer is important, but those who demonstrate its importance by responding to the call to pray. They will prove to be teachable and the best leaders.

Look them over, like a shepherd, while listening to the voice of the Spirit. There may not be among them the most noble of your congregation, the supposed key leaders. In fact, you may have relatively unknown, unproven leaders, yet, folks who are hungry for God. Without being the least bit judgmental, listen to them pray. Chat with them. They may be the raw material that when discipled in prayer would provide surprisingly fresh leadership for the congregation.

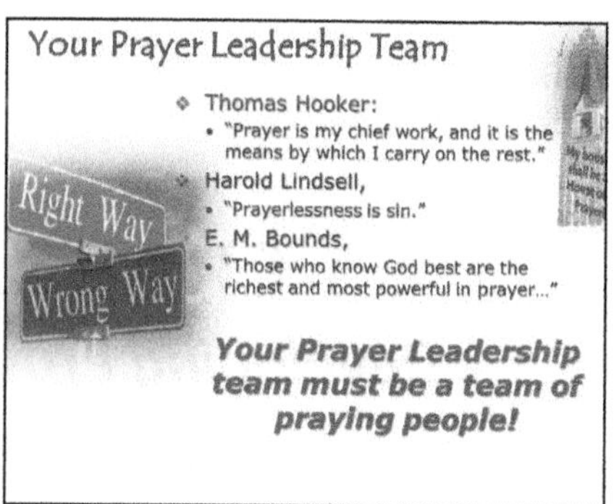
Your Prayer Leadership Team
Thomas Hooker:
"Prayer is my chief work, and it is the means by which I carry on the rest."
Harold Lindsell,
"Prayerlessness is sin."
E. M. Bounds,
"Those who know God best are the richest and most powerful in prayer..."
Right Way
Wrong Way
Your Prayer Leadership team must be a team of praying people!

From the prayer-interested group, those who consistently show up at prayer meetings, select a smaller group who might develop into a prayer leadership-learning team. The operative word is 'learning.' Offer to meet with them monthly to explore prayer concepts and prayer ministry ideas. You want to do this for at least a year. Simply invite them into a learning process. Make it informal. Share. Probe their interest. After some time, ask them what they believe the church would look like if it brought prayer more clearly to the center of all you do, in short, if you moved toward becoming a 'house of prayer.' Spend time praying together as a group.

As you continue to meet with the group, allow it to expand and contract. At first, make the atmosphere relaxed, casual and unceremonious, then grow in the level of commitment required. Some may leave; others may join the effort, always by invitation. But soon, you should have a sense that you are developing a core of potential prayer leaders. Don't hurry the process. Let it develop naturally. Build relationships. Pour into the small group without making them the pastor's pets. Enjoy the ride. You will make a mistake if you attempt to do this as a church-wide training effort. Be selective and allow those who feel called, who keep showing up for prayer, to self-select by their hunger and passion. It is not merely conceptual material that needs to be taught. A group dynamic needs to emerge. Something needs to be caught. Relationships need to be forged. A church-wide class is too formal. Too open. Too random. Make this effort a targeted, by-invitation, off-the-radar, endeavor at developing your select core of prayer leaders.

DISCOVERY MOMENT: Review the resource for an Envisioning Evening in *The Praying Church Resource Guide* available at www.alivepublications.org.

If you do nothing else as pastor with these potential prayer leaders other than model a life of prayer and cultivate a climate of prayer among them, you will be well on your way to success. It is not prayer technique that is the most important element, it is the creation of a culture of prayer, hearts bent toward prayer. And, in that culture, you develop humble, holy, teachable leaders.

Developing Prayer Leaders

It is not merely the material that needs to be covered, it is group dynamic that needs to emerge. It is relationships that need to be forged. A church-wide class is too formal. Too random. Too open. Too random. Make this effort a targeted endeavor at developing a core of leaders.

- Allow the group expand and contract.
- At first, make the atmosphere relaxed, casual and unceremonious, then grow in the level of commitment required.
- Soon you should have a developing core of potential prayer leaders.
  - Don't hurry the process. Let it develop naturally. Build relationships.
  - Pour into the small group - You make a mistake, if you attempt to do this as a church-wide training effort.

Meet with them monthly. Learn about prayer together. Explore, talk, pray together, share. With this team, under the radar screen, quietly 'explore' ways to expand the prayer buffet of your church. Let the group expand and contract. You may lose some and gain others. You may need, at some point, to reconfigure the group. Test commitment. Keep praying together. Dream together. Stretch their understanding of prayer.

You need a 'prayer trainer' in your congregation more than you need a prayer leader. But you need a 'trainer' who is teachable. Having a trainer is a tremendous asset, and being a trainer, getting training, provides the needed boost of confidence and resources to lead the congregational prayer effort. Connect to *The Prayer Trainer's Network* at www.projectpray.org.

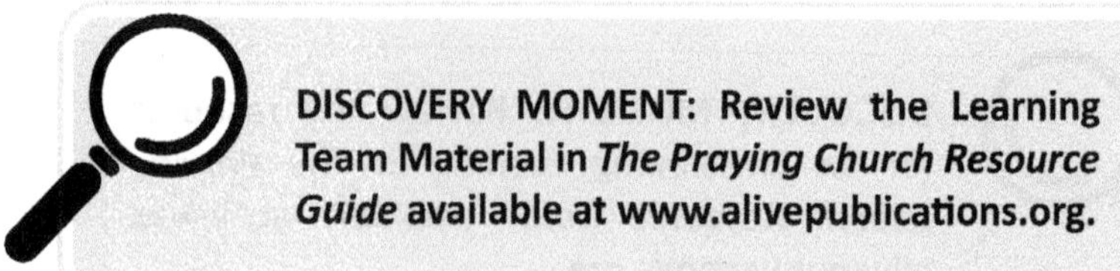
DISCOVERY MOMENT: Review the Learning Team Material in *The Praying Church Resource Guide* available at www.alivepublications.org.

The average prayer leadership team falls apart three times before it gels. Don't get discouraged. Some potential leaders will have very strong but limiting views on prayer. They will have a passion for a specific aspect of prayer – intercession, devotional prayer, faith and prayer, healing, spiritual warfare, prayer for missions, etc. – all noble. Find a place for them. Utilize their passion for the specific, but work on teaming, so that each compliments the other in the prayer process. But don't allow your effort to be narrowly constrained by their theology of prayer or their lack of teachability. Along the way, keep extending selective invitations for others to join the learning group. Look for those who can see the bigger picture. When you feel you have your leaders at the table, and you have learned and grown adequately, learning should evolve to planning. And planning to leading.

During your season of learning, before you move into planning, focus on values – and remember, values are not what we *say we believe*, but what we *do* that demonstrates importance. Core values are praying together, humility and unity, a hunger for the holiness of God, a passion for revival and souls, fruit (character) and fire (enablement of the Spirit). See the values section in this publication and in the *Praying Church Resource Guide.*

DISCOVERY MOMENT: Review "Understanding Mission, Vision, and Values."

As you move forward, you should find in the learning-leader group a growing appetite for new and varied prayer experiences. Don't avoid stretching and unique prayer options. Keep pace with the hunger of the group. Continue your church-wide prayer meeting and perhaps other congregational prayer engagement opportunities. Include special Sunday prayer moments and other church-wide prayer offerings (Special Prayer Emphases). But always come back to your small, potential-leaders group and evaluate. There, you are testing discernment and teaching them to evaluate prayer styles (See chapter two, "Prayer Meeting Styles" in this volume). Allow this group of leaders to expand and contract. Discovering any particular prayer calling of each member. Test them. Challenge their thinking; be gracious, of course, but you want to emerge with a group of teachable leaders with appreciation for a variety of prayer styles and emphases, and an understanding of how to complement one another.

As you pray and learn together, your prayer values will crystalize, your prayer vision will expand, your differentiation between mere prayer tactics and a prayer strategy will become clearer, and the concept of teaming will be more apparent. Out of that will emerge a prayer plan for your congregation.

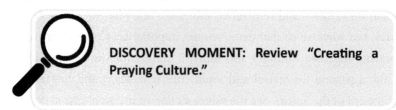

DISCOVERY MOMENT: Review "Creating a Praying Culture."

Qualities Desired in Prayer Leaders

Here are the qualities we are looking for in prayer leaders:

1. **Teachable Leaders** – ready to learn and able to teach others.

   The apostle Paul learned from Barnabas, arguably much less astute than himself, and he learned from the team of prophet-teachers at Antioch, among whom he is listed, but last. He learned from the layman who first introduced him to the gospel, Ananias, no scholar but a sincere man. He taught Timothy and Titus, and we know from his letters that he then encouraged Timothy to teach others. Apollos learned from Aquila and Priscilla, and they may have learned from Paul. We all have something to learn from others, and we are the best teachers when we are first learners.

   If prayer is anything, it is about transformational knowing and learning – and there are no prayer experts.

2. **Role Models** – in prayer and prayer leadership.

   Richard Burr, in his book *Developing Your Secret Closet of Prayer,* reminds us that, "A dynamic praying church is built from the inside out..." He emphasizes four levels of prayer. These are different from the four dimensions that we focus upon in our model for building the church as a house of prayer, but the ideas are complimentary. Burr's first level is secret prayer, our own prayer closet, indicating our personal

Paul writes to the Corinthians, *"Be imitators of me, as I am of Christ"* (1 Cor. 11:1). Here, he establishes the obvious, the horizontal. He says, 'Walk alongside me. I am following Christ. Keep step with me.' It is a simple beginning. To the Ephesians, he offers a higher standard, *"Therefore be imitators of God, as beloved children"* (Eph. 5:1). Now the standard is not only horizontal, but also vertical.

Paul is suggesting, as we learn to follow Christ that we need, both a vertical and horizontal marker. We need human models that are in pursuit of Christ, and therefore, godly examples. Ultimately, that is not adequate. We must see beyond mentors and follow the example of God in Christ. This is a great analogy. Following Christ should produce congruence with peer mentors, tension with godly mentors, should sound an alarm. Like marching in formation, we follow Christ, the leader, but do so conscious of those around us, also following Christ, and in doing so, we keep rank.

Breaking rank means dissonance. We have either switched leaders, and we are following a false Christ; or there is something amiss with the peers with whom we have been walking. They are right - and we are wrong; or they are wrong, and we're the only one right.

There are, of course, times when we might walk alone - but such moments are extremely rare. We follow Christ, we imitate God; and we do so with godly mentors at our side. Of course, we can't imitate God! It is impossible. So Paul would urge, *"Let the same mind be in you that was in Christ Jesus"* (Phil. 2:5). Here is the internal transformation in our thinking. It is beyond invitation. It is the push and confirmation from the inside.

prayer life. This is foundational. Without this primal level, all other efforts at building a house of prayer will fail.

His second level is the family altar – couples praying together; fathers and mothers praying with their children. Prayer must not be strange or foreign to the home.

Third are small groups of prayer outside the home. Triads and quads of prayer. These are focused, small prayer gatherings, prayer cells and the like.

The fourth level is the congregation gathered for prayer – not for preaching or teaching, but simply for prayer.[1]

In *The Praying Church Made Simple,* we are beginning with the end of Burr's model – personal prayer and corporate prayer. In the next phase, we will fill in the middle – couple's praying together and the family altar, both of which are critical, and small groups of prayer, in addition to the corporate prayer gathering. But in the attempt to *simplify* the process, we have suggested that you start with two pieces, not all four.

3. **Peer Leaders** – who will be humble before others, honest before God about themselves, and loyal to the program's objectives.

   We must lead with humility and integrity, without pretense. We must aim to be, as a leader, the first among equals. We lead among, in the midst of others. There can be no lone rangers. Pride is always manifest as standing apart! It differentiates the self – like the Pharisee who distanced himself from others. Pride is aloof, beyond, above, or falsely beneath, but rarely among. Jesus was found *among* the people and His disciples. He was God among us.

   Spurgeon used to say, "We pray best from our depths." That "...the soul had to get low enough to get leverage... and then we can plead with God..."[2] This is about humility. Evan Roberts, the leader of the Wales Revival, would often pray, "Lower, God...take us lower..."[3]

4. **Leaders Committed to the Success and Empowerment of Others** – no toxic prayer leaders. These gatherings will allow you to observe interactions, defensiveness, holier-than-thou attitudes, the one who is like glue to the entire group and the one who seems to prefer some and ignore others. Discourage such relationships. Watch out for power-hungry, know-it-all leaders. Gently prevent abusive relationships. Remember, the disciples had their moments with one another, but Jesus managed to keep them together, and in the end, all of them, but one, became world changers.

In Philippians 2, Paul offers an amazing description of relational health. He cites the need for consolation, for the comfort of love and the fellowship of the Spirit – and with that, he encourages affection and mercy toward one another. These are essential intangibles for a healthy church. Philippians, you will recall, is the epistle with the joint themes of fellowship and joy. Christianity is relational. Paul urges them to be in one accord and of one mind. *"Let nothing be done through selfish ambition or conceit...but in lowliness of mind, let each esteem the other better than himself..."* Wow! The interpersonal view, the posture we take toward another, is the key! A paraphrase might read, "Let each look out, not only for your own interests...but for the interest of others..." The word used here for *others* is *heteros,* meaning the *different* one. It is not *allos*, from which we get *alloy*, referring to metals that fuse or blend well, that easily form a bond. It is not the homogenous, the easy bond with similar people, but the heterogeneous bond, with those who are different in some way – that is Paul's emphasis. We have to work at this unity, reaching out to the one who is the most different and divergent.

5. **Open and Transparent Leaders** – who create a culture for growth, and yet one in which failures and setbacks are celebrated as opportunities to learn, and we lean more heavily on God to deepen them in resolve and determination.

   Prayer keeps the eyes of the group not merely on the program, and not on the problems encountered, but on the possibilities – and ultimately on God. We work to foster a positive environment, an encouraging group with steadfast tenacity to succeed.

6. **Facilitators as Leaders** – you want a group capable of learning how to facilitate peer learning, who are willing and able to learn from others.

   F. B. Meyer was a great English preacher and pastor. He was the founder of the Higher Life Movement and a crusader against immorality. He was a friend of D. L. Moody. Meyer exhorted his people, "Fall on your knees and grow..." Meyer wrote over 40 books and, before his death, he became a global influencer.[4]

7. **Affirming Leaders** – that easily believe in the potential of others, who can see flaws and, beyond them, fantastic possibilities.

   "Albert, you will never amount to anything..." his elementary teacher told Einstein. How could she know that he was distracted because he was under-challenged? D. L. Moody, the great evangelist, did not qualify for church membership on his first attempt. He was too biblically illiterate. Yet, his global ministry lived on after his death, and even today his impact is still felt. He had a disdain for counting converts. No one knows exactly how many he influenced to follow Christ. In just one crusade, some 10,000 people responded.

   We write people off too easily. Who knows, sitting in your prayer meeting and potential leaders group may be a world changer! By the way, Moody had the humility to reapply for membership. He was teachable. He applied himself. He did not succeed by remaining untaught. Affirm and challenge. Inspire the best out of one another. Who can know the power of one potential prayer leader at your table?

8. **Envisioning Leaders** – who help define dreams – leaders call dreams out of you! We should have this effect, one on the other.

   Our goal in prayer is to move from a focus on "the things that break our hearts" to the "things that break God's heart." (Margaret Gibb)

9. **Creditable Leaders** – you want your leaders to grow. You also want them to be recognized as leaders, as successful in the eyes of others. No one will follow a leader in whom he lacks confidence. They may have to rise up, grow into such stature, and you may have to enable that process. In the beginning, they may have to have some relational collateral to launch whatever portion of the prayer effort they lead. Borrowing

your credibility will only get them an opportunity. Then they will have to prove themselves as credible leaders. That is often a process.

10. **Sincere Leaders** – they should not have a hidden agenda. The word *sincere* in the Greek New Testament has an interesting word picture about it. It means to be *without wax.* The idea is rooted in the practice of unscrupulous mediocre sculptors and artisans, who would finish their projects by waxing the external surfaces. To the naked eye, the wax was undiscerned. It made the artisanship look expert. The unsuspecting buyer took the work home and proudly displayed it. All was well, until or unless the work was exposed to heat sufficient to *melt the wax* and reveal the cover-up. Sincere meant to have *no wax,* no hypocrisy, no pretense. It was a 'what you see is the real deal' posture with others.

DISCOVERY MOMENT: Read "The Value of Unity."

Learning Qualities Desired in Potential Learners

There are also qualities necessary in the learners. What should we ask of them? And what should their expectations and requirements be? If you are invited into the potential prayer leader's group, do this:

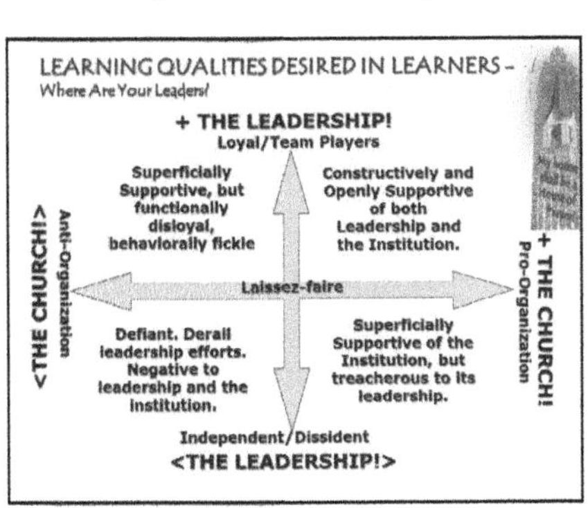

1. Ask God to give you a *good relationship* with the pastor, the prayer trainer and others in the group.

2. *Concentrate* on developing yourself and assisting the learning process in whole group toward your and their potential. Don't expect the pastor or the group to do the hard work for you.

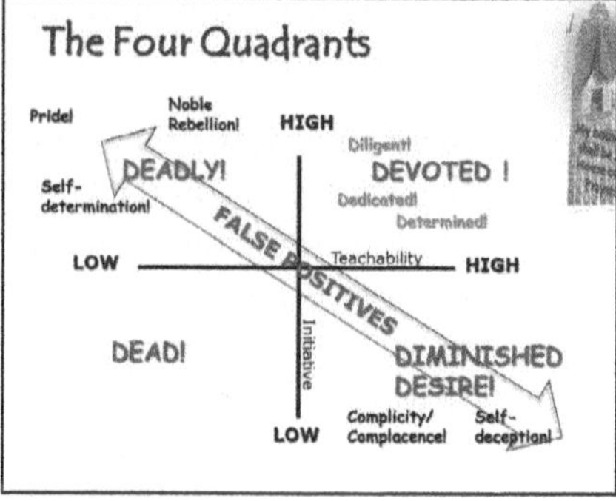

3. Demonstrate a *healthy loyalty* – not only to the pastor, but also to the group.
4. Go to each meeting as a sincere and *open learner.*
5. Go to each meeting with a *focus on helping* someone else in the group – as appropriate.
6. Go to each meeting with *humility,* ready to submit to analysis, objective assessment, to see blind spots through the eyes of others.
7. Go to each meeting with a *contribution* to make to the vision of others.

ACTION STEP: Complete the Rating Sheet: Qualities Desired in Prayer Leaders

Let me say it differently and bluntly. Here are the Seven 'L's for Good Prayer Learners.

1. LOVE GOD – and PRAYER. If you are invited by the pastor to meet with him and others, to explore how to intensify the prayer effort in your church, enter the process with a deep dependence on God. Ask God to give you a good relationship with the pastor as you mentor and with the others in your group.

2. You can't be LAZY; you must INVEST in the experience. You can't ask others to do for you what only you can do. So, concentrate on developing yourself and contributing to others toward the potential of the group. Don't expect the pastor or the group to do the hard work for you.

3. Be a LOYAL member of the learning team. Demonstrate a healthy loyalty – not only to the pastor, but to the group. But at the same time, be honest. Don't come to the meetings to simply placate the pastor. He needs potential prayer leaders to emerge from this group.

4. LEARN – Be OPEN/EAGER TO GROW AND LEARN – Go to each meeting as a sincere and open learner.

5. Determine to LIKE OTHERS – Be FOCUSED on their growth and development – Go to each meeting with a focus on helping someone else in the group – as appropriate.

6. LOWER YOURSELF/Be HUMBLE – Go to each meeting with humility, ready to submit to analysis, objective assessment, to see blind spots through the eyes of others.

7. LOOK FOR OPPORTUNITIES TO CONTRIBUTE – Go to each meeting with a contribution to make to the vision of others.

Let's say it again: Love God, don't be lazy, be a loyal friend and team member. Learn, make learning your goal, and show appreciation and affection for others at the table, even if that means taking a lower posture yourself. All of us need a dose of humility. Look for opportunities to contribute and to help others shine as well.

In Os Hillman's book *Change Agent,* he cites data that claims it takes "less than 3-5 percent of those operating at the tops of a cultural mountain to actually shift the values represented on that mountain."[5] According to Randall Collins in *The Sociology of Philosophies,* a relatively small number of elites have shaped civilizations. In all the social networks, the different culture/social spheres, the number of world shapers, major and minor players, in recorded history is about 2,700. Of those, some 150 to 300 have shaped our world in the last 2,500 years.[6]

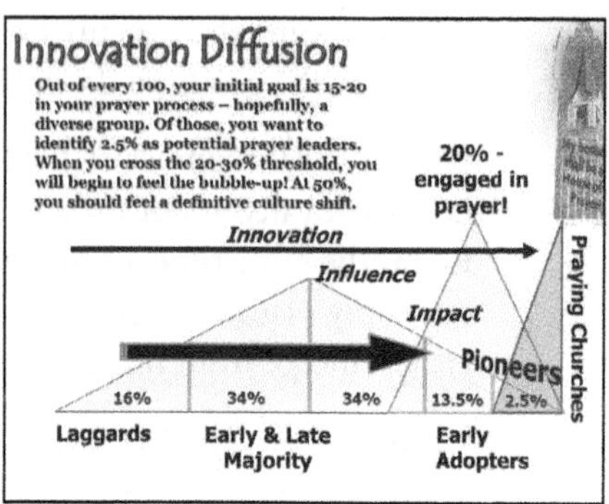

Don't try to influence the entire congregation by a steady, relentless, Sunday morning prayer engagement campaign. That is the wrong leverage point. Don't get discouraged that you do not have Sunday morning attendance levels at your prayer meeting. The benchmark, in the beginning, for your weekly prayer meeting is 15-25 percent of your Sunday morning attendance, and that consistently, before you will begin to feel the impact. The benchmark for this group of learning leaders is three to five percent. These are Hillman's 'change agents' in your congregation. Here you are looking for the 'prayer pioneers' (pioneer is not an age indicator, but an innovation yardstick).

ACTION STEP: Complete the Rating Sheet: Leadership Prayer Survey.

---

1 Richard Burr, *Developing Your Secret Closet of Prayer* (Chicago, IL: Moody Publishers, 2008), 19.

2 C. H. Spurgeon, *Spurgeon's Sermons on Prayer* (Peabody, MA: Hendrickson Publishers, 2007), 259.

3 Jim Cymbala, *Fresh Wind, Fresh Fire* (Grand Rapids, MI: Zondervan, 1997), 131.

4 Quoted by Robert Smith, *Keep Me and Keep All* (Maitland, FL: Xulon Press, 2011), 254.

5 Os Hillman, *Change Agent* (Lake Mary, FL: Charisma House, 2011), 8.

6 Ibid; See also: James Davidson Hunter, "To Change the World," *The Trinity Forum Briefing*, Vol. 3, #2, 2002.

GROUP TALK

1. Make a list of potential prayer leaders who are teachable and willing to meet with you to explore a prayer ministry in your congregation.
2. Look at the list. In terms of your role, use the check list to measure yourself.
3. Where are the areas you most need to grow?
4. Attempting to be objective, use the potential leadership checklist to help you make your decision about choosing your leadership team. Anything you need to add to the list?
5. Rethink the power of a small, committed core in light of Os Hillman's data on change agents.

MILESTONE TWO

Things you should have in place now!

1. Your **PRAYER MEETING** should be continuing, even if it is small and fledgling, up and down in attendance, still looking for its legs. Stay at it. Stay at it, even if you end up having a meeting with the important four – you, the Father, the Word, and the Spirit. Don't give up! Yes, realistically, if the effort is consistently failing, do a forthright evaluation.

Persevere. Remember, Gethsamane – with exception of Jesus – was a prayer meeting failure; but it led through the cross, to the resurrection. What followed was the greatest prayer meeting of all time – the Upper Room. Bad prayer meetings get better.

2. **Develop a PRAYER LEADERSHIP-LEARNING TEAM. Start looking for potential prayer leaders.** Don't be guilty of a narrow stereotype. Pay particular attention to those who have been faithful at the prayer gathering. Remember, 'not many noble and mighty, it is the humble that you seek.' That may include a young, but teachable, relatively new convert, even a young person. You want the perceived mature leaders of the church, but go with the goers.

   The benchmark for your prayer meeting is 15-25% of your Sunday morning attendance, and that consistently, before you begin to feel the impact. The benchmark for this group of leaders is 3-5%. Here you are looking for the 'prayer pioneers' (pioneer is not an age indicator, but an innovation yardstick).

   Choose this group, handpick them, but allow the Holy Spirit to add to the group. Don't announce the formation or existence of this group from the pulpit; do this under the radar screen. You are not ready to 'go public' with a new prayer initiative. You are digging up foundations, laying the groundwork for a future prayer effort. First, you need a better theology of prayer, and a prayer ministry philosophy that fits your situation. And that means teachable prayer leaders. If others want to join, allow them a place at the table.

Once you have peace about your core group of prayer explorers, make the process more formal, gathering them monthly to pray together, consider new prayer models, share stories, do research, watch videos. In some cases, the more the merrier is not the better decision. You are going to need to reshape thinking here, and you need to develop an atmosphere where that kind of transformational thinking is possible.

CHAPTER 6

Advancing on Two Legs: Learning and Doing

The three simple simultaneous processes – personal daily prayer, the church gathered in prayer, and the development of prayer leaders – are your critical first steps.

As you do those things, you move forward on two legs – *learning* and *doing!* First, corporate prayer and second, meeting with your learning leadership team. At those times, you are *learning* – you are growing in your understanding of prayer and of prayer ministry, and you have a small group taking the journey with you. *Doing* prayer, at this stage, by far, is more important. You *catch* prayer. You *learn* to pray by praying.

Jesus took His disciples away to pray. But there were also moments when He unwrapped principles about prayer. Not all is caught; some things are taught. The 'what' of prayer (What is prayer? What does praying do? What does an hour of prayer look like? What do you actually do when you pray? What is intercession, warfare, watching?) is experienced in the 'how' of learning to pray. That is, as you pray, the more you will grow in your understanding of prayer (the 'what' and the 'how'). But the 'why' of prayer will be understood in discovery moments possible only on the other side of shared prayer experiences, beyond superficial knowledge. Unless you are developing leaders to expand your prayer effort, leaders that understand the 'how' and the 'why' of a diverse approach to prayer, the effort will eventually fail; you cannot develop prayer leaders without ongoing, constant prayer experiences laced with teachable moments.

The Linear Cycle

Eastern thinking is cyclical; Western is linear. In truth, we move in cycles that intensify. Think about the development of your prayer ministry as an intensifying spiral. Do prayer, corporately and personally. Then, with a handful of leaders, some of whom may come and go, reflect on your prayer effort. Learn together. Explore. Then, press further into experiencing prayer. Your goal is not the exotic. It is the development of patient, persistent, faithful attendance at the altar, individually and as a group. Think of the small group with whom you are meeting as those who care for the altar, tend the fire, carry out the ashes and lay fresh wood on hot coals. A fire has to be nurtured and fed. The group should reflect on their experiences; learn new ways to pray, and then pray; then relearn, as the leader-pastor teaches into the learning gaps. *Learning* and *doing* are the two legs on which the prayer ministry moves forward.

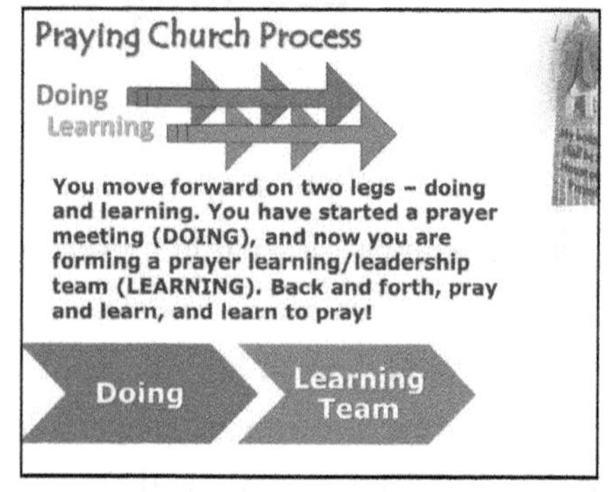

> In the 1960s, when IBM was an up and coming company, an executive made a damaging decision. It ended up costing the company $10 million — and that figure is not adjusted for inflation. Tom Watson, the CEO, called the employee to his office, asking, "Do you know why I've asked you here?" He gave the anticipated answer "So you can fire me!" Watson was surprised by the response. "Fire you?" he responded, "Of course not. I just spent $10 million educating you."[1]

First, we have to *teach* our way out of what has become a narrow, self-interested view of prayer. Sound Bible teaching and preaching champions the value of daily time with God, the importance of prayer as a central spiritual discipline, the consequences of an undisciplined spiritual life, the value of time with God for the sheer pleasure of His Presence. It sees prayer not merely as acquisition or the exchange of things, but prayer as relationship, as the exchange of persons – the heart of which is love, and the goal of which is holiness. This kind of teaching is priceless and irreplaceable. People perish for 'lack of knowledge.' Yet the transition into richer and deeper prayer is not a matter of head, but of heart – and that involves action.

"The single biggest problem in communication," wrote playwright George Bernard Shaw, "is the illusion that it has taken place." George Barna, the church researcher, found that the typical church member cannot remember the theme of a sermon two hours after the church service.

Our praise and preaching services are doing little to impact the thinking, much less the behavior of our people – and beyond that, we are losing the entire culture, since only 17.7 percent of the population is in church on any given Sunday! We must move beyond preaching and teaching, even training, to implementation. In short, to discipleship and the integration of prayer principles into life action.

Preaching on prayer will gain general agreement – it is important. There are few things more important. At the beginning, the enthusiastic response is often, "We need to pray more, Pastor! Amen." When you call a prayer meeting, however, the 'amen' corner is often too silent, and few – if any – show up! However, this can be good, even if it is painful because you now have the true measure of the people's value of corporate prayer and the level of hunger for prayer. You have determined your base-line for growth. Only a fool determines that being embarrassed by such a dismal few turning out to a prayer meeting is more important than building a praying church. Denial is not an option. Don't cancel the prayer meeting due to a lack of interest. If you do so, you have just closed the church! Persist.

In the early years at Central Church of God, a mega-church, Loran Livingston, Senior Pastor, tells the story of his father-in-law, a veteran pastor, issuing a call for an all-night prayer service. As midnight drew near, he and his father-in-law were the only ones in attendance. Another hour went by. His father-in-law dutifully paced the floor of the sanctuary, praying and praising, clapping his hands and interceding. Loran recalls stopping him. "You mean, me and you are going to do this all night? Even if no one else comes?" The important One was there – the Lord. They persisted. I have been in prayer gatherings at Central that drew a thousand or more for the sheer purpose of prayer. Persist. Be patient.

Start the Process

Start small. Here is the early benchmark – 20 percent of the Sunday crowd at your congregational prayer meeting. It may sound too small, like a truncated vision. Of course you want more. Of course you want your Sunday morning crowd or its equivalent. But first, you need a group of healthy Christians who realize the importance of seeking God. You need a group that is willing to learn a variety of prayer styles. You also need a group that demonstrates consistency and persistence. You need a group with resolve, to whom God has begun to communicate His promises regarding the congregation and the community.

Of the approximately 320,000 Christian churches in the US, the median gathering is 75. Let's say you have 75 in attendance on Sunday morning. You are then the typical USA congregation. Half of all churches in the US are below 75, and half are above. A congregation of 350 or more is in the top ten percent. We are a nation of small churches – and small churches can be both healthy and effective. As a typical church, if your prayer gathering is averaging 7-10 people, upwards to 20 at times – rejoice. Take in the lows and highs. In fact, don't worry at first about numbers. Establish consistency. Faithfulness. Emphasize the priority of time with the Lord. That means you may show up, and keep showing up, with no other human in attendance. Heaven, however, notices such faithful perseverance and rewards it.

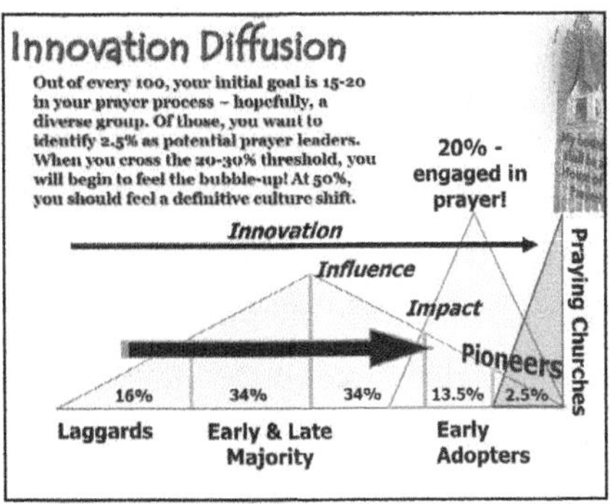

DISCOVERY MOMENT: Review the "Prayer Meeting Styles" in Chapter Two of this book.

When people do gather, engage them in a variety of prayer styles. Your goal is not to be exotic! You must know the wineskin with which you work and how much the people long for fresh wine, and the degree to which they are capable of stretching. Don't break them, but do stretch them. Depending on the prayer customs of your congregation, allow time for folks to pray alone, then in small groups, but don't force prayer style changes. Take small steps. Wait on the Lord. Walk the sanctuary. Pray aloud, together, then one at a time. Use prayer stations or banners. (Order banners at www.alive-publications.org.) Keep the prayer gathering within the time frame of 60-90 minutes. There may be exceptions to this, but generally, the rule is to keep the fire within the altar. So you set boundaries. If a passion for prayer extends beyond the time you announced, allow those with hot hearts who want to tarry to do so. Release the others. "We've reached the time that our prayer service was to end. The Holy Spirit is obviously not finished with some of us. Others may have obligations that force you leave – we understand. We bless you. Leave as you need to do so." There should be no guilt; it is a lousy motivator. Those who absolutely have to leave will appreciate the blessed release.

Make special prayer for specific needs a part of the service, but not the main thing! If personal 'prayer requests' and the like begin to dominate the prayer time, it will generally kill the prayer service. The prayer time cannot be allowed to become narrowly focused on personal needs, even legitimate and desperate needs. Our personal needs should find their place in the larger kingdom focus to which prayer must continually rise. The need for 'daily bread' and inner emotional distress and 'deliverance' from some work of the Evil One is invited, but always in the scope of the larger, *"Let thy Kingdom come, thy will be done!"* context of prayer. Keep the focus on praying for the in-breaking rule of God into our time-space world, for His triumphant hand to be seen, for the glory and power of His kingdom to manifest, for submissive hearts that seek to both know and do His will – the smaller needs will be taken care of in the scope of the larger prayer focus.

Say to the people, if necessary, "If you have special needs, specific prayer requests, we'll have a time at the end to anoint each of you and pray with you and for you." The wounded or weary lamb is not to be scolded or belittled for coming with needs. But we will not help the weak among us if we perennially allow self-obsession to triumph. Keep the focus on growing in Christ, praying the promises, missional prayer for awakening in the city, on some nation that you have adopted as a prayer focus. Pray for the lost. Pray the newspaper. Pray for needy sectors in the culture. Allow time for folks to pair up and pray for one another. Above all, spend some time modeling scripture praying.

There is a time and a place for a pastor, like a shepherd, to move among the sheep, for whom he is called to care, and lay healing hands on them in prayer. This is the essence of the work of the pastor-shepherd – watching and praying, not merely preaching. The pastor who preaches to his sheep but does not systematically and persistently pray for them, may be a good talker, but not a shepherd.

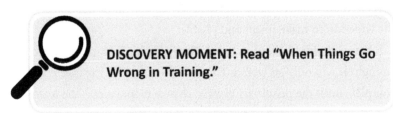

DISCOVERY MOMENT: Read "When Things Go Wrong in Training."

Teaching and Training

As you begin to pray together, you will discover issues where people may be reluctant to go in prayer, you may discover prayer styles and practices that, unaddressed, will cause your prayer effort to stall! You want to teach and preach into these learning gaps, but not usually during either the prayer meeting or the Sunday morning service. This kind of teaching is best done with a shepherd heart in a small group or one-on-one. Some correction may be needed when unhealthy beliefs and behaviors occur, but do so gently. Don't correct from the pulpit something that happened as a sidebar event in the weekly prayer gathering.

The teaching and preaching in mind here are things the Holy Spirit will point out as needs for congregational growth – for example, you may see the need to address the relationship between faith and prayer; why praying in the 'name' of Jesus is important; the Bible as a prayer book; the power of blessing; certain aspects of spiritual warfare – the list goes on and on. You'll notice these things as you pray together – the number of people who show up at a prayer meeting without a Bible, since they have no clue about the relationship between prayer and the Word; the number of people who cannot verbalize prayer, since they have no understanding of the power of 'speaking the promises,' of praying aloud – and some may have been taught that silent prayer is the equivalent of spoken prayer, or that saying a prayer aloud gives Satan some advantage. Your prayer process will be loaded with land mines of superstitious thoughts and ideas, traditions and styles that have become sacred and stiff. As you observe these barriers, gently teach, pouring the oil of the Spirit on the wineskin to make it soft and pliable.

You will also discover that teaching/preaching on prayer is not enough. It will only get you as far as nodding heads. The task is not complete until the people are given a chance to 'practice.' The learning is proved in the doing; not even in the reciting of the principles, but, rather, in the practice. Preach and teach, then practice. Then teach into the learning gaps. Then practice again.

You teach it and then do it. The prayer ministry moves forward on these two legs. *Doing* prayer and *learning* more about prayer; then *learning* and *doing* it – applying what is learned. And all the while, *developing leaders.*

DISCOVERY MOMENT: Read "When the Prayer Effort Explodes."

Getting Unstuck

Ask yourself: Why do people listen to a message on prayer and seem engaged, and then not show up for prayer meetings? Is it because they are disinterested? Eighty-four percent of people who call themselves a Christian pray every day. Some more than once a day. Now, these tend to be fleeting prayers, but they cross a wide spectrum of issues. People pray mostly for health and safety (78 percent), for strength for the day (75 percent), for relationships (68 percent), for finances (55 percent), and many pray for others who are suffering (42 percent). Amazing, 76 percent pray for God's forgiveness and 93 percent for His guidance – people want God to be involved in their lives and in the lives of others. Forty-four percent pray for those who do not have a relationship with God. Seventy-four percent pray that they themselves will have a stronger faith. Ninety-one percent say they regularly whisper thanks to God. This does not sound like a disengaged people. So why do they not come to our prayer meetings?

First, we have privatized faith. People tend to think that these private prayer moments are adequate. They do not understand the Biblical power of praying collectively as the church and doing so from the office of the church. So, we need to emphasize the Biblical authoritative importance of corporate prayer, of agreeing together with others in prayer, of the power of the prayer meeting. Second, people fear the prayer meeting itself. They don't know what to expect. They are not sure they will be comfortable. They are fearful that they might be asked to pray – out loud. They are uncertain of their own spiritual strength and status with God. They feel inadequate as a prayer warrior; they can

> We must stop using the fact that we cannot earn grace (whether for justification or sanctification) as an excuse for not energetically seeking to receive grace.[2]

pray, but they reason that prayer meetings belong to the realm of some spiritually elite group. Third, they are content with a light, pray-as-you-go-along-life's-way prayer life. They have not cultivated a deep transformational prayer habit, personally or corporately.

Don't interpret the low attendance at a prayer meeting as a lack of interest. Probe. Inquire. Remove the barriers. You do this by bringing prayer to them – front and center, Sunday morning. You do this gracefully, gently and lovingly. Let them experience God in prayer. And then invite those whose interest is peaked into a deeper prayer life.

Don't interpret the low attendance at a prayer meeting as a lack of interest. Probe. Inquire. Remove the barriers. You do this by bringing prayer to them – front and center, Sunday morning. You do this gracefully, gently and lovingly. Let them experience God in prayer. And then invite those whose interest is peaked into a deeper prayer life.

Your prayer meeting is *the* meeting in which you grow people. They are not passively listening to preaching, they are engaging God about those principles that have been preached. You want prayer-engagement that is transformational. But, you do not want your prayer meeting to be intimidating, as if only for veteran intercessory Christians. There is a tension here and the appropriate balance can only be established by the leading of the Holy Spirit, probably, context-by-context. You need intercessors and their passion. Forty percent of the psalms are 'lament' psalms – passionate, tearful praying. But, not all of these psalms were public laments. Establish a healthy prayer balance.

Here are some ideas for moving forward:

1. *Create a climate that is inviting* for everyone – even for the new convert to learn to pray.

With all due respect to the core intercessors and with a deep appreciation for their intensity and passion in prayer, you may have to distinguish between gatherings strictly for intercessory prayer and a call to the general church to pray. The goal is neither to shield people from intense intercession, nor to make an intense intercessory style a model for your prayer gatherings. Clearly, at least in some cases, at some times, intercessors pray differently than those who do not have the same call to prayer or have little experience in prayer beyond a fleeting intercessory plea. Intercessors are already underappreciated. So we should never minimize them or their contribution. Yet, intercession is not the center of prayer; it is the missional edge of prayer. It is transactional, doing business *for* God and doing the business *of* God. Petition, prayer requests, are transactional as well. The center of prayer is transformational – worshipful prayer.

You may need to teach your intercessors to distinguish between what is appropriate in the delivery room and what is appropriate in the lobby, in the general prayer arena. Here is the bottom line – create a prayer environment that welcomes veteran intercessors along with newcomers to corporate prayer, and one especially welcoming to new converts. Throwing them into the deep end of the prayer pool may not be the best way to initiate them into prayer. However, keeping them out of it will also be a mistake. This is not a call to *seeker sensitive* praying, but a call to wisdom and balance.

2. *Focus on relational, transformational prayer.* Don't make your prayer service all about praying for needs. The more important point is seeking the 'face' of God, praying for personal transformation. Create moments to pray with and for one another. One-on-one pairings are very intense. Groups of three to five allow the more timid a bit more interpersonal space. Prayer circles of five or more become impersonal. Larger circles may discourage first-time pray-ers.

3. *Don't leave people to themselves all the time.* If you do, you end up with individuals praying in the same room and thinking you have had a corporate prayer experience. A

group of individuals doing their own thing in prayer is, at best, collective individualism. It is not a prayer army. An army moves together in a disciplined, ordered manner. We sometimes have a prayer mob, but not a prayer army. So, give direction to the prayer experience. Give the people a focus for prayer. And send them into prayer, but then call them back and unite them around another focus. Corporate prayer is not having individuals praying, even fervently praying, in the same room; corporate prayer is the group praying together.

4. *Use the Bible as a prayer book.* Find Biblical principles in a passage and use those as a guide for prayer. Prayer needs structure. The psalms are largely a collection of prayer – and they have structure about them. The ideas in them move. They can be divided into different genres of prayer – prayers of order, disorder, new order; pleas for mercy; courtroom prayers; imprecatory prayers; pleas for forgiveness; all of which have about them distinctive components – structure.

5. *Have a plan for your prayer meeting.* Most pastors have learned that is it best to go to the pulpit having prepared to preach or to lead people in the study and reflection of Scripture. However, we would be impoverished were it not for the wonderful moments when God interrupts and changes the order of things. At such times, fresh inspiration is infused into the study prepared by the leader, and as a result, people are fed with manna from on high. In the same way, a shepherd needs to know the meadow to which he wants to take the people in prayer, the high place that he feels led to invade or the treacherous mountain pass that the congregation needs to navigate that is best approached first by prayer. Have a plan, and then, in the context of prayer, yield to the leading of the Holy Spirit.

6. *Record significant moments and movements in prayer.* In the book of Acts, we find the recorded content of a prayer meeting (Acts 4:31). Or, we find a record that captures the experience following prayer (Acts 2, 3, 4, 13, 15). At times, we are given the content that was prayed or the content

that emerged from the time of prayer. Keep a record of the church's prayer meetings, especially breakthrough moments, special insights, promises God gives, warnings. A corporate prayer journal may be the most important record that a church keeps.

DISCOVERY MOMENT: Take another look at "A Glimpse of Prayer in Acts."

7. *Remember, prayer is the means by which we navigate life.* It is the means by which the church advances. We move from order, through disorder, to new order! God speaks when we seek His face. And at times, there is a message even in His silence. He provides direction when we lean on Him. The hinge of change, the edge of breakthrough or breakdown, is always found in and around prayer gatherings. Stay alert. Listen to the Holy Spirit. Someone needs to discern the voice of God out of these gatherings: "What is the message of the Spirit to the congregation?" Whatever that message is, the congregation needs to know it and affirm it.

Prayer Service Plan

10-15 minutes	Thanksgiving, praise and worship
15-20 minutes	Praying scripture
15 minutes	Intercessory prayer - for the lost, the nations, for mission
10-15 minutes	Personal needs
5-10 minutes	Thanksgiving

ACTION STEP: Complete the Rating Sheet: The Seven Indicators That You're on the Right Track.

People are willing to be taught about prayer, hear stories about answers to prayer – indeed, those are exciting – and, at times, they are willing to receive the prayer support of others. But when you move from *learning* to *doing,* participation often falls precipitously. Don't let that stop the process. Avoid the trap of thinking that *teaching* on prayer is the same as *doing* prayer! *Learn – and do!* Learn and test the learning by practicing it.

The handful of folks with whom you are quietly and regularly meeting is your primary test group. They should be exploring prayer and prayer ministries. This group should include any existing prayer leaders and perhaps interested intercessors, even staff or key lay leaders, those who demonstrate their desire to learn about prayer or new ideas for implementing a prayer ministry in your church. Don't condemn those who don't appear interested or refuse to participate – those who do and don't respond to the call to pray often surprise pastors. Go with the goers. Also, don't allow those who see no need to explore new prayer models and learn new prayer concepts to take the process hostage. Some may see no need to acquire new practices of prayer: "What's to learn about prayer?" There is, of course, much to learn. The learning process is humbling – and that is the best medicine for prayer leaders. Level the ground. There are no prayer *experts.* In the class called "Prayer 101: Knowing, Relating and Talking with God," everyone is a student.

This team will learn together, pray together and at some point begin to explore what prayer ministries might look like in your church in a year, in two years, in three years – eventually. You may utilize them in leading a variety of different prayer activities. Still, they are a 'learning' team.

DISCOVERY MOMENT: Read "Humility and Prayer."

What you now want are both Learning and Doing

Continue to have your prayer meeting. Don't stop. Don't make this group *your* prayer meeting either. After a season, with increased interest, add to the weekly prayer meeting wider church prayer experiences! And don't forget those Sunday morning prayer moments at least once a quarter or more often.

With your small learning team, 'explore' options for expanding prayer ministry. Keep learning. Here are some suggestions for the learning process.

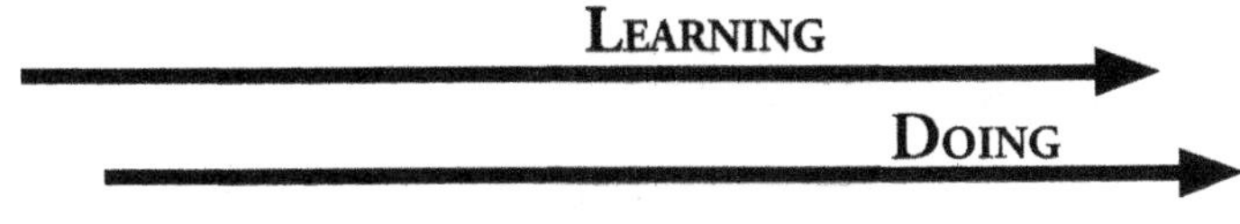

Learn:

- PRINCIPLES – teach on prayer! New learning!
- PRACTICUM – what those principles look like applied. How is this practiced? Make your teaching practical.
- PICTURES – give stories, examples and illustrations.

Do:

- Let's pray! Prayer walk. Explore. Practice. Do it.
- Keep asking, where are we in the process?
- Keep evaluating, do you now have a persistent core?
- Are you able to teach into the learning gaps? Does the group receive correction with grace?
- What are your biggest hurdles? Successes?
- How is the prayer meeting going? Are you reaching five percent of the Sunday morning crowd? Good start. Don't give up. Keep praying. Ten percent? Twenty? Now you are really gaining traction.

- Expect ups and downs. And don't miss the message in the 'down' times. Don't react, but do read the moment – assess.

Remember again, the absence of steady participation is not always an indication of disinterest, but of fear. And sometimes, spiritual drowsiness. The only option is to keep praying while the others sleep; God will awaken them. Also, teach to instill confidence, then do prayer with confidence! And then teach into the learning gaps.

The small developing leadership group should have several immediate goals. These components guide the learning team meetings:

1. To PRAY together. Perhaps a novel idea, but if any ministry is to be birthed from prayer, it should be the church's prayer ministry itself. Prayer is the nexus of vision. In prayer, the creative Holy Spirit births new ideas.
2. To LEARN together. They should consider reading and studying together, sharing new insights and ideas about prayer ministry.
3. To EXPLORE together. They should look for living examples of prayer ministry models. Interview folks near – pastors and prayer leaders – who have a vital and active prayer ministry. Learn from those who have traveled the road. Learn. Adapt. But don't merely copy. Superficial adaptation of the ideas of others is tactical, not strategic. Import only the models that are consistent with your values and philosophy of prayer ministry.
4. To PROJECT. From their discoveries, this team needs to project what prayer ministry should look like in their congregation. This includes: exploring vision and values; the congregational mission as it relates to prayer; how prayer interfaces with the whole life of the church.
5. To MODEL. All the while the group meets (monthly, at the very least), they should also be participating in the congregational prayer activities, if not leading some of those experiences.

Genuine believers, those with the indwelling Spirit, want a deeper personal relationship with God. At times, you have to 'wake up an overgrown heart,' but once awakened, they hunger for God, but still lack confidence in approaching Him, and beyond that, in being used of Him to minister to others or to the city.

The Long View

This is not a sprint – it is a marathon. To change the culture of a church, you have to change the habits of its individual members and families. That is a marathon.

As your leadership team meets, lace in prayer moments. Remember, if it is not a praying team and is <u>**not open to learning**</u> – ***the prayer ministry will fail.*** And if the prayer leadership team *does not become a praying team* – the prayer ministry will fail. If they pursue the *pieces* of the prayer ministry about which each of them is passionate without a seamless approach to prayer, without regard for the whole – the prayer ministry will fail. If they do not have a clear and long-term sense of where the prayer ministry is to take the church, namely, to revival and mission out of personal transformation, then the prayer ministry will fail and competitive prayer options will emerge. If they are not humble, a non-negotiable essential – the prayer ministry will fail! Prayer should change the *ethos* of the whole church. Here are some additional long-term markers for your journey. These are meant to help you keep the long-term view in mind.

Five Long-Term Markers

1. <u>*Keep the Big Picture in mind*</u>. In the early stages, frequently review the '7 Markers' and the 'Ten Values of a Praying Church.' Envision your future. Dream. Think strategically.
2. <u>*Constantly Assess*</u>. Are we doing what we have learned? If so, we really learned it! If not, teach and train into the learning gaps.
3. <u>*Celebrate small victories!*</u> See the challenges, but don't see them alone.

4. *Be guided by your developing plan.* Don't be tempted to chase a new rabbit that crosses your path! Don't substitute small programs for large purposes.

5. *Be sequential*. Exploit the power of sequence. This is the difference between the tactical (one small piece/program/activity) and the strategic (linking those pieces together). You are building a house of prayer. Be strategic. So you teach, then do. Practice with small groups, and then take the process to the whole congregation. Fit the parts together.

DISCOVERY MOMENT: Read "Creating a Praying Culture."

Beyond the Three Simple Steps

Your ultimate goal is to mobilize an entire church to pray. At first, everyone will say, "Yes, let's make our church a house of prayer!" Then the reality of what prayer costs will become clear, and your initial enthusiasm will fade. Don't be discouraged. Persevere without being punitive toward those who pull back – you'll have some surprises in this area. Refuse to allow a "they don't want to pray!" pessimism to develop among your leaders. It is a subtle form of pride that will paralyze your movement. It leads to a division that immobilizes you. There can be no *them* and *us* mentality allowed to take root.

Your prayer journey is much like a long interstate trip. There are many entrances and exits along the way. Some will leave you and later rejoin the movement. Others will not come into the stream of prayer initially. They may choose another entrance point. For example, not all will respond to an all-night prayer meeting. The idea may be too intimidating for them. Some intercessors may not want to be a part of an 'Intercessory Prayer Team.' Not everyone will attend the church-wide prayer gatherings. No single prayer slice, program or event, will capture everyone. Some will join the parade through the entrance of the prayer evangelism effort. Others may join when you announce prayer training for lost family members. Still others, when you form prayer ministry teams. Some will see a need for family prayer, for learning to bless their children, and that will be the key to their response. A few will join you in support of national concerns and moral issues. Some may have a specific passion to pray daily for Jerusalem. If you expect everyone to come through one door, one event, or one training model – your prayer process will fail. It must be broad and long-term. Keep offering different entry points into the journey.

This means that you have to create side doors into prayer. Even tually, your prayer leaders will work with department leaders to help them integrate prayer into every aspect of the life of the church, so that all your congregational members will inevitably be exposed to new prayer styles and models, literature and language. Don't expect all your church members to come to you – to either your prayer training, learning or doing events. Take prayer to them. You will eventually, but not in the beginning, integrate prayer into every seam of church life. This will happen as the leaders of Sunday School classes, small groups, men and women's ministries, children and youth leaders, couples and singles – all are trained themselves as prayer leaders. Insist: To be a

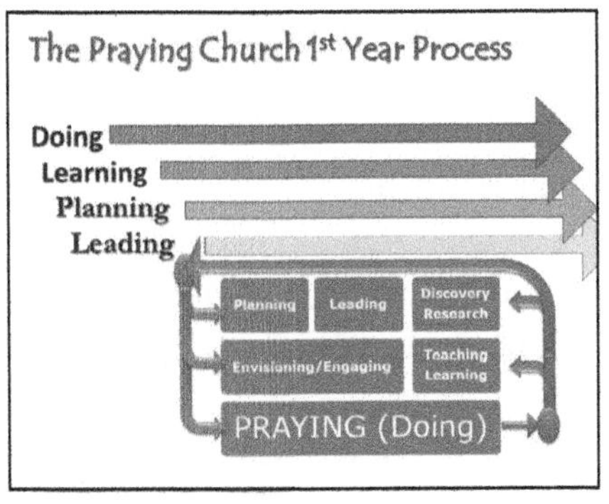

leader of any ministry in this church, you must be a prayer leader.

At first, you may do random prayer experiences based on arbitrary interests, unsystematic exploration. But eventually, you need to move from a casual tasting of different prayer models to a more intentional approach. And that means supporting your 'doing' with 'learning' by intentional 'leadership.' You want to sequence those – you have to 'lead' the development of your prayer ministry. You teach/learn; then you lead/do; and then you teach/relearn/lead in correction. And that means, at points, unlearning. You address the learning gaps and compliment the positive, learning/leading. Here is an example of sequential, strategic planning:

Example

You conduct:

(1) a prayer evangelism training event in order to	[learning and doing]
(2) create prayer evangelism teams, which must be subsequently carefully appointed and functioning for	[leaders – trained leadership] *(duly authorized)* [doing – applied learning]
(3) the coming church-wide emphasis on prayer and mission,	[a wider learning/event]
(4) after which you will plan to expand your teams and choose your wisest and most intuitive people as leaders of prayer evangelism teams as preparation for the	[leadership: assessment] (restructuring)
(5) community evangelism festival, at which your church will provide leadership in modeling prayer	[doing *out of learning* – you

evangelism for other churches,	want a proven team here] [others can learn by observation – junior team leaders]
(6) after which you will regroup to assess,	[leadership function]
(7) teach into the training gaps and	[re-learning]
(8) launch another level of recruiting and training not only in your church, but now for the city, all for the purpose of	[learning]
(9) putting together a training team for	[leadership broadened]
(10) ongoing ministry in your church and as a service to other churches in your area.	[broadened doing] [broadened teaching and training]

These 'tactical' pieces gain power as they are laced together as a part of a larger strategy. You are *learning* to *do, training* leaders, then executing. Assessing, then re-teaching, at times restructuring. Each event builds to another, but the subtext is equally important – mobilizing trained and confident workers. Ever broadening both circles – the leadership team, the trained team members and participants/recipients.

Like a chain, one weak link threatens the integrity of the whole chain. The power of your prayer ministry will not be in one single area, but in how you link the strength of each area together.

---

1 Chip Heath and Dan Heath, *Switch: How to Change Things When Change is Hard* (New York: Broadway, 2010), 173.

2 Dallas Willard, quoted by James. C. Wilhoit, *Spiritual Formation as if the Church Mattered: Growing in Christ through Community* (Grand Rapids, MI: Baker Academic, 2008), 77.

GROUP TALK

1. Take a moment and think about the learning–doing tandem and how you might apply that in the next three months.

2. Pray about how you will launch your process. Settle the issue – the fact of the prayer meeting and the act of the prayer meeting are more important than the size of the prayer meeting.

3. Pay attention to what you pray about. What your congregation prays about. Ask God for guidance in altering the prayer focus and stretching prayer styles.

4. Review the seven suggestions for moving forward.

5. Use the five goals of developing prayer leaders to build your learning group meetings. A suggested model:

   7:00 Prayer

   7:15 Learning (Start with the Learning Team Material.)

   8:00 Exploring/Brainstorming – Sharing Models/Ideas

   8:15 Projecting/Planning the Practice of Prayer

   How can we integrate prayer into the fabric of our church life (small prayer groups; family prayer; personal prayer; prayer retreats; prayer walks/missions; youth/children's prayer, etc.)? The assignments might be: Meet with the choir director before the service, and gather a few others to pray for him/her. Arrive early and pray in your Sunday School class; find one other member each week, call them and pray with them, etc.

8:30 Pray together – and Commit to Model Prayer.

6. Review the *Five Long-Term Markers* for your journey. After each of the learning team meetings, ask yourself – *Did we…?*

7. Review the sequential model – notice how you dance through the learning–doing–leadership–training areas. These *four quadrants* all must be firing done in some rhythm. The absence or ineffectiveness of any one is deadly to your mission. Lay out a sequence that involves learning–teaching (concepts: what), include meaning (why), make it practical (how: skill, confidence), then lead it, do it, practice it, apply it. And do that with your eyes wide open. Make sure you have the ability to adapt (leadership – what if?). Then assess and teach – start the process again.

ACTION STEPS

1. Develop a learning plan for your prayer leadership team. Project the critical topics and ideas you want to review in this first year. (Consider the *Learning Team Material* in the book, *Prayer – The Heart of It All.)*
2. Brainstorm creative ways to lace prayer more fully into congregational worship experiences.
3. Consider the 'style' of the congregational prayer meeting. Will it be relational or traditional? What Biblical passages could you use to teach your people to pray the scripture?

PERSONAL PRAYER

CHAPTER 7
The Habit of Personal Prayer

Prelude

John Welch was born around 1570, near the dawning of the Reformation. His youth was so troubled that his father said he expected to hear that he had been hanged as a thief. When he was saved and called to ministry, he was country crude with a prophetic edge. His custom was to preach daily after spending a third of the day in prayer. In the city of Ayr, around 1590, he had a difficult beginning. The area was so ungodly and wicked in its ways that no one would provide housing for a preacher. Division and faction triumphed along with often bloody conflicts, so that the streets were not safe. Welch would throw himself between angry parties, even after the men commenced a fight. Soon, the city saw that he was an agent of reconciliation, and, little-by-little, he made the town a peaceable habitation. This is gospel engagement, not withdrawal.

For Welch, it was not enough to end the fighting. When a skirmish was over, he brought a table into the street, set the enemies down, prayed and persuaded them to profess themselves to be friends, and then they ate and drank together. He ended the affair by singing a psalm. The whole town came to observe these peace encounters, and after a season, they listened more closely to his ideas, and they grew to respect him. He became the necessary town councilor, the settler of disputes, and the arbitrator of peace, without whose advice the people would do nothing. Soon, they were imitating him.

When, before preaching, he felt weak, he would call for prayer before ascending the pulpit. Those who knew him noted times when he left the city to seek solitude for seasons of prayer and occasions when he prayed through the night. Even though he traveled some distance from town, he gave himself so fully to prayer that his voice would find its way into the streets. Men and women would hear the sound of the preacher's cries in prayer for them.

The Sunday habit of the folks at Ayr, and at least one clergyman, were Sunday games of amusement. Welch hated the practice. He felt it profaned the holy day. One man's house was a center of such activities. Welch wrote him several letters expressing his concern, which the man ignored. The preacher's heart was not settled on the issue, so one day he showed up at the wealthy man's gate and informed him that because he had not heeded the warning and would not restrain the profane activities on the Lord's day, that he would lose his house and none of his children would enjoy the inheritance. Soon thereafter, the man's fortunes reversed. He was forced to sell his estate. When he surrendered the property, he confessed to his wife and children that he found Welch a true prophet. Indeed, the hard way.

Short term pain has more impact on most people than long-term benefits do.[15]

Welch married Elizabeth Knox, the daughter of the famous

John Knox, minister at Edinburgh. The couple had three sons, and they knew great loss. The first was a doctor, who was innocently killed by accident. Another son was lost at sea; his ship sank. He swam to a rock and survived, only to starve for want of necessary food and refreshment. When his body was found, it was in the posture of prayer, upon his bended knees, with his hands stretched out. The third son, Josias, carried the grace of his father, and was minister at Temple-Patrick. He was referred to as the Cock of the Conscience because of his extraordinary passion, his call for spiritual awakening and his rousing gift. Sadly, he too died young. A grandson took up the mantle of ministry.

> You cannot sustain a personal, intimate relationships with the Lord in a group, and yet, because faith is never to be privatized, because He has loved us that we might love one another and has called us into fellowship with others, you cannot satisfy your obligation to God with a purely private prayer and devotional life. And you cannot satisfy your relationships with God on the back of public, corporate prayer.

John Welch, it is said, abounded and excelled most in prayer. He wondered how a Christian could lie in bed all night and not rise at some point to pray. He rose often in the night to pray, and he knew the art of watching in prayer. One night, his wife became concerned, fearing he might catch cold. She found him earnestly praying, "Lord, wilt Thou not grant me Scotland?" and, after a pause, "Enough, Lord, enough." She inquired, "What did you mean, 'Enough, Lord, enough?'" He was reluctant to answer her, and only revealed that as he had wrestled with the Lord for Scotland, he became aware that a sad and difficult season would soon be on the nation, but there would be a remnant. The revival he longed to see would not come in his lifetime. One man, a former parishioner who later entered the ministry, recounted a night that Welch had tarried in prayer, indeed, one in which he was for a season, watching in prayer. Friends were waiting on him and growing weary because of his long stay. One of them caught a glance at Welch in prayer. He reported a strange light, an aura surrounding him, and he heard him speak strange words, evidencing his spiritual joy.

The admirers of Welch knew his holy life, his pastoral abilities and, particularly, his prayer life. They knew the impact, the success of his ministry in the town. The minister had gained great respect. When the great plague raged in Scotland, Ayr was immune. The whole countryside was infected, all around them. The magistrates had posted guards to prevent the plague from being carried into the town. One day, two merchants sought entrance. They had with them a load of cloth upon a packhorse and wanted to offer their goods for sale. The sentinels stopped them and called the magistrates, who promptly called the pastor. Welch took off his hat, greeted the traveling merchants, and then lifted his eyes to heaven. He uttered no audible prayer, but he didn't hurry the process. He continued in a prayerful posture, and after a season, he advised the magistrates to forbid the merchants to enter, that the plague was in their packs. Upon his advice, the magistrates commanded the travelers to be on their way. Twenty miles away, they entered the town of Cumnock and sold their cloth there. The town was so devastated that the few living who remained were hardly able to bury their dead.

Welch became more than a preacher; he became a kind of oracle. He remained humble and enjoyed the fellowship of the whole town. His ministry ended with the sad thing he had seen in prayer, the destruction of the Church of Scotland by King James. Welch called it the edifying of the Church by its suffering. Among the number persecuted by King James was John Welch, who was accused of treason and incarcerated. He was carried as a prisoner to Blackness Castle, then sent to Edinburgh Tolbooth for trial. And then from prison to prison, till he was banished to France, with the intent that he would never see Scotland again.

While he was in Blackness, he wrote his famous letter,

> Who am I, that He should first have called me, and then constituted me a minister of the glad tidings of the Gospel of salvation…and now, last of all, to be a sufferer for His cause and kingdom. Now, let it be so that I have fought my fight, and run my race, and now from henceforth is laid up for me that crown of righteousness…

In defiance of King James, he declared, "Christ is the head of His Church…[and] she is free in her government from all other jurisdiction except Christ's…" It was for this reason, the idea of a free Church, the notion that God's sovereignty was expressed in the Church, and stood above the Crown, that he believed he was being held as a prisoner.

> We have been ever waiting with joyfulness to give the last testimony of our blood in confirmation thereof, if it should please our God to be so favorable as to honor us with that dignity…I do affirm…all other things which belong to Christ's crown, scepter and kingdom, are not subject, nor cannot be, to any other authority, but to His own altogether.

He noted that he would be "glad to be offered up as a sacrifice for so glorious a truth," and such a moment would be "the most glorious day, and the gladdest hour I ever saw in this life…"

He wrote to Sir William Livingstone of Kilsyth about the Archbishop of Spottiswoode,

> We are sure the Lord will never bless that man, but a malediction lies upon him…I am far from bitterness, but here I denounce the wrath of an everlasting God against him, which assuredly shall fall, except it be prevented. Sir, Dagon shall not stand before the Ark of the Lord…[he] will have a fearful end.

The prophecy was literally accomplished. The Archbishop died in a foreign country and in misery. His son was beheaded. Welch was a prophet, without the benefit of the title. Walking the streets of Edinburgh, before his arrest, as a national crisis regarding the church emerged, Welch minced no words. He named two more preachers who he said were no great friends to Christ. Both died. After he became a prisoner, he sat at a table and shared fellowship with other imprisoned believers. One young man took a sharp exception to his remarks, laughed, and sometimes mocked Welch, with the habit of making sarcastic faces. One day, Welch suddenly changed moods, and all the company became quiet. He turned his attention to the young cynic, and the entire group watched the young man melt in his seat, sinking down. He slipped from the chair and died under the table.

Lord Ochiltree was in charge of the compound where Welch was held as prisoner and was, in fact, related to him. Welch asked if he could preach the gospel. Lord Ochiltree was reluctant, but promised to put the proposal before King James. However, when he had an audience with the King, he found King James raging against preachers, and he decided it would be vain to inquire; however, he told Welch that King James had not provided a definitive answer. It was a lie. "Nay," Welch told him, "My Lord, you should not lie to God, and to me; for I know you never delivered it, though I warned you…because you have dealt so unfaithfully, remember God shall take from you both estate and honors, and give them to your neighbor in your own time." He lost both his estate and honors.

His wife attempted to remain near Welch while he was in prison. Longing to see her family, she made a trip to Ayr, but he warned her not to take the ordinary way, specifically, not to pass the bridge into town, but to cross the river above the bridge. The cause for caution? He informed her, "You shall find the plague broken out in Ayr." In crisis, the people again appealed to him, but Welch directed them to Hugh Kennedy, a godly gentleman, who he said, should now pray for them. Kennedy, known himself as a mighty wrestler with God, gathered a number of citizens and prayed earnestly. And the plague ceased.

After Welch was deported to France, banished with five other preachers, he applied himself and, in just a bit more than fourteen weeks, he was able to preach in French. His ministry would continue there for sixteen years.

Bible Reading Guides

- **Old/New Testament** — Each day includes a passage from both the Old Testament and New Testament.
- **Chronological** — Read the Bible in the chronological order in which its stories and events occurred.
- **Beginning** — Read the Bible from start to finish, from Genesis to Revelation.
- **Historical** — Read the books of the Bible as they were written historically, according to the estimated date of their writing.
- **Bible in 90 Days** — An intensive Bible reading plan that walks through the entire Bible in 90 days.
- **Read the Gospels in 40 Days** — Read through the four Gospels – Matthew, Mark, Luke, and John – in 40 days.
- **New Testament in a Year** — Read the New Testament from start to finish, from Matthew to Revelation.

Link to these guides at www.biblegateway.com.

On one occasion in France, a young man, whom Welch deeply admired, fell ill and died. He was removed from his bed and placed on a pallet, but Welch, in great grief, remained with him for three hours, lamenting over him. Twelve hours later, the coffin arrived. But Welch asked for additional time, another twelve hours. The weather was hot, and the men became impatient, demanding that the corpse of the noble young man be placed in the coffin and speedily buried. But Welch earnestly begged them for additional time. The corpse had now remained on the pallet for thirty-six hours, and then he begged for yet another twelve hours. After forty-eight hours had passed, Welch still held out against them. Friends began to believe that perhaps the young man was not dead, but strangely subdued by some apoplectic fit. They suggested a trial by doctors to see if any spark of life might be found. The physicians went to work. They pinched him in the fleshy parts of his body. They twisted a bowstring about his head with great force, but there was no sign of life. The physicians again pronounced him dead. No more delay was to be afforded. Incredibly, Welch begged them to step into the next room for an hour, perhaps two, and leave him with the dead youth's body. Amazingly, they acquiesced to his request.

Welch fell down before the pallet and cried out to the Lord with all his might. He stared at the lifeless body, continuing to wrestle with the Lord. He persisted. The dead youth opened his eyes and cried out, "O sir, I am all whole, but my head and legs." Those were the places that the physicians had so mercilessly pinched, attempting to arouse him. Welch presented the dead young man restored to life again.

With war in France, Welch's wife petitioned the king that he might return to Scotland to breathe native air. The king was, at first, indignant to her request, but inquired about her background and history. When he discovered that she was the daughter of John Knox, he was unsettled. "Give him his native air?" replied the King, "Give him the devil!" She persisted. Finally, the king told her that if she would persuade her husband to submit to the bishops, he would allow him to return to Scotland. Amazingly, Mrs. Welch lifted her apron and replied, "Please your Majesty, I'd rather keep his head there." Welch did return to London, but he languished there. He longed to preach, and after additional petitions, that right was granted. It was to be his last sermon. He preached long and with fervency, and after he had ended his sermon, he returned to his chamber and within two hours, quietly and without pain, resigned his spirit into his Master's hands. Of his preaching, it was said that no one could hear it and not weep.[1]

Such stories are intimidating. Yet, they offer hope – that ordinary men and women, who are deeply dependent on God in prayer, can change cities, plant churches and impact nations.

DISCOVERY MOMENT: Read Prayer Fundamentals.

The Habit of Daily Personal Prayer

As a pastor or prayer leader, the group you lead will rarely rise above your personal prayer life. Pray by yourself, for yourself and others. Start meeting with God daily. Embrace the discipline of prayer. In fact, only in those personal moments will you gain the grace and insights to lead the public component of prayer. And you will learn that public prayer, no matter how passionate and fulfilling, can never take the place of private prayer times with the Lord. You will also discover that public encounters with God will drive you to find private space to seek God further. If you are going to lead prayer – you must pray!

Leonard Ravenhill thundered,

> No man is greater than his prayer life. The pastor who is not praying is playing; the people who are not praying are straying. We have many organizers, but few agonizers; many players and payers, few pray-ers; many singers, few clingers; lots of pastors, few wrestlers; many fears, few tears; much fashion, little passion; many interferers, few intercessors; many writers, but few fighters. Failing here, we fail everywhere.[2]

ACTION STEP: Complete the Rating Sheet: Ten Assertions of Prayer

Pastors and Prayer

A study conducted for LifeWay Christian Resources of Protestant church pastors revealed that only sixteen percent were *very satisfied* with their personal prayer lives. Some 47 percent were *somewhat satisfied.* That means that 63 percent were to some degree satisfied, while 30 percent were somewhat dissatisfied, and seven percent *very dissatisfied.*[3] Bottom line, at least from one perspective, is that even with the moral chaos around us in the culture, the church in free-fall, barren altars, conversions that are little more than the repetition of the words of a prayer, almost two in three pastors are okay with their prayer life! Unbelievable. Do we fail to see the connection between the lukewarm church and pastoral prayer? That the central role of the shepherd is *watching* the flock, a metaphor for *prayer?* Even with the current dismal state of affairs, moral chaos among spiritual leaders, a lack of passion in the pulpit and the pew – almost two of three clergymen do not see the problem as related to their prayer life.

The study revealed significant variations by age – just nine percent of younger pastors, those 45 or under, were *very satisfied*; along with 13 percent, ages 45 to 59. Thirty percent of those 60 or older were content with their prayer lives. Younger pastors are actually more likely to be very *dissatisfied* with their prayer life than they are to be *very satisfied.* That may be good news. Interestingly enough, there was little variation due to denomination or theology.

Pastors were asked how long they prayed each day, and that number was about 30 minutes daily, up from previous data (the mean is 39 minutes, half praying more, and half less). Although younger ministers expressed more dissatisfaction with their prayer lives, they spend about the same amount of time in prayer as their older peers.

They were also asked about their focus in prayer. One-third of their prayer time is spent in offering prayer needs to God. Another 20 percent in quiet time, listening to God; then 18 percent in thanksgiving, 17 percent in praise, while 14 percent is spent in confession. That translates to 12 minutes a day offering prayer requests, eight minutes of quiet soul time, seven minutes of giving thanks and another seven in praise, with about five minutes in self-examination,

> The gospel orients us not so much to an object, as to a person. The Gospel, then, is not so much belief <u>that</u> as it is belief <u>in</u>.[16]

repentance and confession – clearly not enough emphasis on transformational growth and change. Its presence, if only two to five minutes, is perhaps one of the more encouraging aspects of the report.

When pastors were asked about specific prayer topics, most revealed a long list of issues for prayer. About 90 percent had prayed for members of their congregation, for the spiritual health and growth of the church, as well as for wisdom in leading their church. That did not necessarily mean a focus on numerical growth. Things pastors were least likely to pray for included church and personal finances, for other Christian leaders, including those in their own denominational circle. Even persecuted Christians in other countries had trouble making the pastoral prayer list. Mainline denominational pastors were more likely to pray for their denomination than were evangelicals (57 percent to 34 percent).

The biggest difference, according to the study? Those who are more satisfied with their prayer lives spend more time in prayer than those who are not (56 minutes a day in prayer – very satisfied; 43 minutes – somewhat satisfied; 29 minutes – somewhat dissatisfied; 21 – minutes very dissatisfied). We might conclude, the more satisfied, the longer one spends in prayer. Or we might also conclude, the more time one spends in prayer, the more satisfying prayer becomes.

One other important difference is this: pastors who are more satisfied with their prayer life spend much less time doing either list – praying or in petition, and much more time listening to God. When they venture into petition or intercession, it is usually with a big issues focus, one greater than their own life or congregational issues, for example, overseas missions, the persecuted church, outreach and evangelism. They pray for other churches and pastors in their area, for global events, for the nation, for specific Christian leaders along with government leaders, and they intercede for their denomination or stream of fellowship.

According to Ron Sellers, president of Ellison Research, who conducted the study,

> What drives a satisfying prayer life for a minister is spending less time asking God for things and more time listening to what God has to say, praying for issues beyond their own personal and church needs, and spending much more time overall in prayer…These are not minor percentage differences in the study, but major ones – 78 percent of pastors who are very satisfied with their prayer life had prayed recently for overseas missions, compared to just 40 percent among those who are very dissatisfied with their prayer life, for example. These numbers are hard to ignore, and it would be unwise to do so.[4]

Renewing Pastoral Respect in the Culture

If there is one common denominator that characterizes great Christian men and women, it is a cultivated and persistent life of personal prayer, extraordinary prayer mingled with brokenness, out of genuine humility; decorated with power from heaven to make a difference.[5] Calvin Miller observed, "Preaching, in one sense, merely discharges the firearm that God has loaded in the silent place." The real power of preaching is in praying. Eloquence is not enough. Articulation and learned speech methods may please a crowd, but they will not change hearts, and hell does not fear them. As Ravenhill noted,

> Satan has little cause to fear most preaching. Yet past experiences sting him to rally all his infernal army to fight against God's people praying…The pulpit can be a shop window to display one's talents; the prayer closet allows no showing off.[6]

When this country was founded, clergy were among the primary forces who drove the Revolution. Called 'the black-robed regiment,' they spoke out concerning the issues of the day. These pastors were critically instrumental in America's winning their independence. Wearing their clerical black robes, they entered their pulpits preaching

Ways to Structure Your Prayer Time

- Prayer that Jesus taught (The Lord's Prayer) – In Matthew 6:6, Jesus gave a model of a private prayer life. Read more in the previous article, 'Creating a Personal Prayer Room.'
- A.C.T.S. – This is an easy way to remember key elements of prayer. It's simply prayer in four parts: adoration, confession, thanksgiving and supplication (petition; needs).
- Psalm 17 – A prayer model based on each verse: Invoke the privilege of hearing: 1-2; Confession/Profession: 3-6a; Specific petitions: 6b-9; Report – a situational assessment: 10-12; Plea for intervention: 13-14; Resolution: 15.
- Tabernacle – The tabernacle is a template for prayer and worship, a roadmap into God's Presence, a call for balance in prayer and worship. Learn more at www.alivepublications.org/product/principles-of-worship-a-study-of-the-tabernacle-of-moses.
- Praying the Psalms of Order and Disorder – READ a small portion of Scripture. REFLECT. What one verse, phrase or word stands out? REASON/WRESTLE. What does this mean? To me? Enter into a dialogue with God over your open Bible. Meditate. Question. Gasp! Stand in awe. REST. Quiet yourself for a Word from the Lord! BECOME. Let the Word form you!

Note: The book, *The Prayer Closet,* has models for personal prayer, practical information for creating a prayer room. There is a Resource Kit also available with Teaching Guide. www.alivepublications.org/shop/the-prayer-closet.

about justice and the political process. They were fearless as they expounded, week after week, principles rooted in Scripture, along with the proper role of government and responsible citizens under the Lordship of Jesus Christ.

In central Carolina where I live, the Piedmont area was still a wilderness in the mid-1700s. Local history records that as people moved into the area, coming up from coastal Charleston or coming down the Great Wagon Road from Pennsylvania, which was barely

> John Stott argued, "Holiness is not a condition into which we drift."[17]

more than a rough and untended path, they settled within a few miles of one another. And then collectively, they sent for a preacher whom they mutually supported. He became the cultural expert, the tutor for their children, the man who cultivated community values, and the glue that held them together. He was respected and revered as a man of prayer and character. Without a church building, they designated a well-known tree as a Sunday meeting place, brought a picnic lunch, had a service with communion, songs and prayers. As they casually spent the day together, they shared recipes and news. When they could afford to do so, they built a church around which community flourished.

In a recent poll, Americans were asked what group of professionals they felt contributed 'a lot' to the well-being of our society. The military topped the list at 78 percent, quite a change from the Vietnam era. They were followed closely by teachers at 72 percent and doctors at 66 percent. Scientists and engineers scored 65 and 63 percent respectively. But clergy, once the most noble of the professionals, the most revered, by contrast, garnered a score of only 37 percent. Just a bit more than one-in-three felt that ministers contributed 'a lot' to society. Shocking. Journalists and lawyers were a bit lower. Even white evangelical Protestants only gave the clergy a 52 percent rating; white Catholics, 47 percent; and white mainline Protestants, 46 percent. When the category 'contribute some' was combined with 'a lot,' the numbers for clergy rose to 72 percent for the general population and a bit higher among church goers. That is about the same as the number of cultural Christians in the US. Of the 'unaffiliated,' only one in five saw the benefit of clergy to culture as 'a lot.' Why have clergy lost such respect? The scandals? Cultural disengagement? Cultural wars and value incongruence – abortion, gay-rights, liberal sexuality? Can we attribute the decline in clergy respect to cultural mores and value shifts alone? Or has something about the clergy itself changed in the last fifty years that we have missed?

Prayer Legends

It is always dangerous to put forth the greats in prayer because it tends to make us all shrivel up in intimidation and guilt. Any mature believer knows that grace-based praying is the best gift we offer to God. Prayer, to be effective, must be a freewill offering. It is our *choice* to spend time with God, an expression of our love response to Him. It cannot be a 'have to,' or a duty; but a 'want to,' a delight. Discipline may have to be cultivated for a season and periodically reapplied to stay in spiritual shape. But if the runner hates running, he will eventually quit; if the athlete hates the game for which he is training, he will give it up, the price being too great. And if the pastor does not delight in spending time with the God whom he preaches, he too will fail. Discipline can only be a temporary motivator, then delight must take over! Prayer must be borne by love. The great men of Christian history were in love with God. And their daily schedule showed it. They were not in love with preaching or crowds, with big churches or programs – they were in love with Jesus. And they spent much time alone with Him. Those private moments marked them with His glory when they stood before a crowd.

It is said that E.M. Bounds, whose writings on prayer excel, rose at 4 a.m. daily and engaged in a regular three-hour prayer regiment. Martin Luther admitted, "If I fail to spend two hours in prayer each morning, the devil gets the victory through the day. I have so much business I cannot get on without spending three hours daily in prayer." His motto was, "He that has prayed well has studied well." Samuel Rutherford rose at three in the morning to meet God in prayer.

John Wesley, the founder of the Methodist movement, "spent two hours daily in prayer. He began at four in the morning." Someone noted, "He thought prayer to be more his business than anything else, and I have seen him come out of his closet with a serenity of face next to shining."[7] Francis Asbury, who carried on work in frontier America among the Methodists, noted, "I propose to rise at four o'clock as often as I can and spend two hours in prayer and meditation." The early Methodists prayed 'from four to five in the morning, private prayer; and from five to six in the evening, private prayer." William Bramwell, one of the great holiness preachers of Methodist fame, was noted for living on his knees and then riding his circuit like a flame of fire. He would spend as much as four hours in a single season of prayer.[8] John Fletcher, another Methodist leader, is said to have "stained the walls of his room with the breath of his prayers." He prayed at times all through the night; always, frequently, and with great earnestness. His life was a life of prayer. "I would not rise from my seat without lifting my heart to God." Greeting friends, he asked, "Do I meet you praying?"

David Brainerd, the son-in-law of Jonathan Edwards and missionary to the American Indians, noted in his diary,

> I got up this morning and the Indians were still committing adultery and drinking and beating their tom-toms and shouting…I prayed from a half hour after sunrise to a half hour before sunset. There was nowhere to pray in the Indian camp. I went into the woods and knelt in the snow. It was up to my chin. I wrestled in prayer until a half hour before sunset, and I could only touch the snow with the tips of my fingers. The heat of my body had melted the snow.

Edward Payson was a leader in the Second Great Awakening who became known as 'Praying Payson of Portland.' When they prepared his body for burial, they found thickly calloused knees from his prayer life. He prayed at his bed with such fervency that he wore two grooves six or seven inches long into the hardwood floor. The great Scottish preacher, John Welch, noted earlier, would rise at night and wrap himself in a blanket. His wife would find him on the ground, weeping. He would reply: "I have the souls of three thousand to answer for, and I know not how it is with many of them!" It was said that Welch, whose father-in-law was John Knox, spent four to six hours a day in prayer. Adam Clarke reminds us, "Prayer requires more of the heart than the tongue."

George Mueller funded his orphanage operation on his knees. He refused to go public with his needs or those of the children; he took them to God. He prayed in millions of dollars for the orphans in his care over the years at Bristol, England. John Hyde, the great missionary to India, would tarry in prayer on his face, waiting for heaven's answer. He came to be known as 'Praying Hyde.' He worked as a missionary until his health failed. Back home, a doctor examined him, "Mr. Hyde, do you have any pains in your chest?" "Yes, I do," the missionary admitted. The doctor was forthright, "Mr. Hyde, your heart has displaced itself. Your heart ought to be here, but it has moved over in the cavity of your chest, and that can only happen through one thing – agony." Hyde knew the cause of his migrating heart – intercessory prayer. He was warned to stop whatever was causing such an effect on his heart or he would die; his reply was that were he to stop, he might as well be dead! He became known as 'the apostle of prayer,' and his prayers were arguably responsible for thousands coming into the kingdom of God in India. His heart had moved to the 'right' side.

Adoniram Judson, who labored in Burma, was a prayer warrior as much as a missionary. His goal was to devote two or three hours daily, beyond devotional exercises, to what he called "the very act of secret prayer and communion with God." During the day, he endeavored to withdraw from business and find solitude to lift his soul to God. He began his day shortly after midnight, devoting time amid the silence and darkness of the night to the sacred work of prayer. At dawn, he sought to be in prayer. At nine, twelve, three, six, and nine at night, he paused for prayer. It was a resolution with him – a sacrifice. He allowed neither business nor company to rob his time with God. Such devotion to prayer is regarded today as beyond fanatical – as insane. Dr. Judson worked in Burma, and labored for years without a breakthrough, but he laid the foundation for a work in the nation of Burma. No man can do a great and enduring work for God who is not a man of prayer.

Jesus prayed in the garden until he moved past perspiring, and his sweat became as great drops of blood. James, the bishop of Jerusalem, the brother of Jesus, was found after his death to have knees as calloused as those of a camel. Great men, who do great things for God, have time for God, and they show it by taking time to pray. R. A. Torrey warned, "We must spend much time on our knees before God if we are to continue in the power of the Holy Spirit." Ravenhill charged, "Poverty-stricken as the Church is today in many things, she is most stricken here, in the place of prayer…Failing here, we fail everywhere." Both ministerial vision and passion are tied to the prayer altar. "The secret of praying," the great revivalist urged, "is praying in secret. A sinning man will stop praying, and a praying man will stop sinning. We are beggared and bankrupt, but not broken, nor even bent." And prayer is our capital.[9]

Re-defining a Pastor's Role

There are a three New Testament descriptors for the pastor – *shepherd, bishop,* and *elder*. The latter term, *elder,* references maturity. *Bishop* is a function of oversight, authority and a reference to office or position. But it is the term *shepherd* that is most apt; it is the relational aspect of the role, the heart of the pastor's function – to relate and care for the sheep, to lead them and call them by name, to live with them and know them, to protect them and search for them when they stray, to provide green pastures and still waters, to help them to their feet when they are 'cast down' and to allay their fears (Psa. 42:5, 11). One of the great callings, perhaps the principal calling of all, is to *watch* over the flock. The idea of watching is a metaphor for prayer. We are to 'watch and pray; pray and watch.' The term goes back to the garden where Adam was charged with the responsibility of growing and *guarding* (watching) the garden, of tending it and protecting it. He was to *watch,* and, by inference, to *pray.* Of course, the power is not in the watchman, he is only the lookout. Throughout the Old Testament, the term means watchman, the one on the wall or the one who went about the city, or perhaps the one who lifted his voice in warning (Gen. 2:15). Again, it is a metaphor for prayer. Its parallel term shows up consistently in the New Testament as well.

Timothy Witmer, in his book *The Shepherd Leader at Home,* identifies four foundational functions of shepherding – knowing, leading, providing and protecting.[10] The shepherd *knows* the sheep; this is relational. He *leads* the sheep; this a function of call and gifting, the ability to read the terrain and study the pathway. He *provides.* In the winter, he prepares the green meadows, and in the summer, he leads the sheep to the mountain terraces. In both cases, the shepherd plans ahead. He is not unaware of seasonal changes and the challenges that each brings. He 'provides' and 'protects' in any present moment, but he has also 'prepared a table.' That is a reference to the 'table-land' and the plateaus or terrace – the high country. Finally, he *protects.* He stands between the predator and the sheep or lamb. He risks his own life. The loss of a lamb is personal. He would rather die himself than attend the funeral of one of his own. In *knowing,* he is like a father. In *leading,* he is like a trailblazer. In *providing,* he is a strategic planner. In *protecting,* he is a prayer warrior. He prayerfully watches the flock. In deep dependence on the Holy Spirit, he leads the flock. As God gives him bread, in prayer he provides for the flock. He fights for the flock. Still, the greatest underrated responsibility of the contemporary pastor is watching his flock in prayer!

> Great teachers don't teach. They help students learn. Students teach themselves.[18]

Abraham felt a responsibility for Lot, even if his nephew lacked character and integrity, and when he knew that he was in danger, he implored God to spare not only him, but the wicked city in which he lived. And in that moment of passionate intercession, he gained grace for the city if only ten righteous souls could be found. And when they were not, God remembered Abraham and delivered Lot. Jacob's passion, despite his own sin and defect of character, is a lesson in tenacity in prayer, *"I will not let you go except you bless me."* (Gen. 32:26). He understood the giving nature of God, that true blessing came only from Him, and only in prevailing prayer. When God declared Israel worthy of immediate judgment, Moses, their shepherd, who had his own issues with the people, pleaded with God, *"What about Your reputation? What will the nations say?"* (Ex. 4:1). The holy plea rose above the immediate crisis and staked a claim for the honor of God! And the nation was spared. Nehemiah stood between the broken walls of Jerusalem and God, and was used to do in a matter of days what had not been done in seventy years.

Jesus and Prayer

We should have to look no further than the life of Jesus as a model of a praying shepherd! Mark 1:35 tells us, *"In the morning, having risen a long while before dawn, He departed to a solitary place and there He prayed."* The early hours of the day were marked by time with His Father, and He would operate out of that spiritual strength.

> *At evening, when the sun had set, they brought to Him all who were sick and those who were demon possessed and the whole city was gathered together at the door, and then He healed many who were sick with various diseases and cast out many demons and He did not allow the demons to speak because they knew Him* (Mark 1:32-34)...*Simon and his companions went and searched for Him and when they found Him they said, 'Everyone is looking for you!'* (Mark 1:36-37).

The greater the pressure, the larger the crowds, the more the needs increased, the more Jesus prayed. He insulated himself from stress in the shadow of His Father.

This pattern characterized His whole life. The disciples saw the pattern. In Acts 6, they were feeling the pressure of growing crowds and escalating needs.

> *In those days, the number of Grecian Jews among them complained against those of the Aramaic speaking community because their widows were being overlooked in the daily distribution of food. So the twelve gathered together and said, 'It would not be right for us to neglect the ministry of the Word of God in order to wait on tables. Brothers, choose seven men from among you who are known to be full of the Spirit and wisdom. We will turn this responsibility over to them and will give our attention to prayer and the ministry of the Word'* (Acts 6:1-4).

With the exponential growth of the church came an unexpected pastoral problem. The tension between two ethnically different groups may have been the presenting problem, but it was not the root issue. The problem was a prayer problem. The lack of grace in the church, among the people, indeed between the people, they attributed, amazingly, to a lack of prayer. 'They' were now being perceived as the 'source' of solutions, and their attentiveness to the 'tyranny of the urgent,' rather than the priority of prayer, had created an expectation that was unrealistic. *"We must give ourselves continually to prayer and the ministry of the Word"* (Acts 6:4).

Overview of the Prayer Life of Jesus

He prayed:

- Alone (Mt. 4:23; Mk. 1:35; Lk. 9:18, 22:39-41).
- In public (Jn. 11:41-42; 12:27-30).
- At His baptism (Lk. 3:32-22).
- Before meals (Mt. 26:26; Mk. 8:6; Lk. 24:30; Jn. 6:11).
- Before important decisions (Lk. 6:12-13).
- Before and after healing (Mk. 7:34-35; Lk. 5:16).
- To do the Father's will (Mt. 26:36-44).
- For our unity (Jn. 17).
- He taught on the importance of prayer (Mt. 5:44; 6:5-15; 21:22; 7:7-11; 18:19-20; Mk. 5:44; 11:24-26; Lk. 6:27-28; 11:2-4, 9-13; Jn. 14:13-14; 15:7, 16; 16:23-24).

Specific occasions in which Jesus prayed:

- Lk. 3:21-22 – At His baptism.
- Mk. 1:35-36 – Early in the day, before leaving on a trip to Galilee.
- Lk. 5:15 – After a healing.
- Lk. 6:12-13 – All night, before choosing the 12 disciples.
- Mt. 11:25-26 – While speaking to the Jewish leaders.
- Jn. 6:11 – Before feeding the 5,000 (Also see: Mt. 14:19; Mk. 6:41; Lk. 9:16).
- Mt. 14:22 – Before He walked on water (Also see: Mk. 6:46, Jn. 6:15).
- Mk. 7:31-37 – While healing a deaf and mute man.
- Mt. 15:36 – Before feeding the 4,000 (Also see: Mk. 8:6-7).
- Lk. 9:18 – Before Peter had the revelation in which he called Jesus "the Christ."
- Lk. 9:28-29 – At His transfiguration.
- Lk. 10:21 – At the return of the seventy.
- Lk. 11:1 – Before teaching His disciples what we call 'the Lord's Prayer.'
- Jn. 11:41-42 – Before raising Lazarus from the dead.
- Mt. 19:13-15 – Laying hands on and praying for little children (Also see: Mk. 10:13-16; Lk. 18:15-17).

- Jn. 12:27-28 – In asking the Father to glorify His name.
- Mt. 26:26 – As He instituted the Lord's Supper (Also see: Mk. 14:22-23; Lk. 22:19).
- Lk. 22:31-32 – In the final hours, when Peter's faith wavered, Satan asked to "sift" him, but Jesus prayed for him.
- Jn. 17:1-26 – The great prayer for unity. He prayed for Himself, His disciples, and all believers just before heading to Gethsemane.
- Mt. 26:36-46 – In Gethsemane, before His betrayal, He engaged in three intense seasons of prayer (Also see: Lk. 22:39-46; Mk. 14:32-42).
- Lk. 23:34 – After being nailed to the cross, Jesus prayed, "Father forgive them; for they know not what they do."
- Mt. 27:46 – As He hung, dying on the cross, Jesus cried out, "My God, My God, why hast thou forsaken me?" (Also see: Mk. 15:34).
- Lk. 23:46 – In His dying breath, Jesus prayed, "Father, into thy hands I commend my spirit."
- Lk. 24:30 – Jesus prayed a blessing on the bread before He ate with others after His resurrection.
- Lk. 24:50-53 – He blessed the disciples before His ascension.

The epistles offer glimpses regarding the prayer life of Jesus. According to these passages, He is praying now, making intercession on our behalf (Rom. 8:34; Heb. 7:25; 9:24; 1 Jn. 2:1). In truth, in prayer, we join Him – and pray with Him.

Praying as a Pastor

There is no special power in the prayers of a pastor, only in the prayers of Christ. But there is a special prayer calling bound to the office and function of a pastor, which is in turn bound to role of mediator, and it is rooted in the prayer ministry of Christ. In that sense, prayer is the greatest work of the pastor. And it is difficult work. It is a battle against the world, against the flesh and against the Devil. It is, using the specific analogies of Paul to the ministry of a pastor, the work of a highly trained and disciplined *athlete,* a diligent *farmer* and a determined *warrior* (2 Tim. 2:1-7). The diversity of the images is striking – the pastor as a bearer of seed and cultivator, a nurturer looking for a harvest, while at the same time fighting a battle and staying disciplined – in shape, in order to finish his own race well and obtain the prize. One of these tasks alone is more than sufficient for the energy of even an extraordinary man – but a pastor is to do all three simultaneously, and well. He *runs* his own race, he *plants* and waters and watches for the harvest, while he *battles* unseen spiritual forces. As he *prays*, he plants – and therefore, he *gives* the seed to the ground, keeping himself under subjection *(fasting)*, in shape, lest he run in vain. All three of the primary disciplines that Jesus promoted are present – *prayer, fasting and giving* – and the root discipline is prayer (Mt. 6). It is the work of the pastor which will make the greatest eternal impact. It is the essential work.

The pastor that does not pray for and with his people, who does not *watch* – a metaphor for prayer, meaning that he does not care for his flock in prayer, entrusting each life to God – is no true shepherd at all. He may be a great public speaker, a whiz at running a non-profit, a blast at the mayor's annual barbecue, but he is not a holy man of God. He may love crowds, but the real question is the one Jesus put before Peter, *"Do you love me?"* (John 21:15-17).

It is the relationship of the shepherd with Jesus, the love relationship, out of which the commission is given, *"Feed my sheep; care for my lambs."* A man who is not in love with Jesus is a danger to the church. A man who is not spending time with the Lord can offer nothing but human insight, frail fleshy efforts, comfort that lacks the divine difference that is so obvious when the Comforter Himself is involved.

Such a man is a proud and self-sufficient man who is convinced that his studied words are as effective without God's empowerment as they would otherwise be if they and he had been bathed in dependence on God, evidenced in prayer. Blindly, such a man lacks mercy for his people as well. He offers human compassion, perhaps even tearfully, but he is blind to the fact that the greater need is for the favor and mercy of God's evident compassion by the touch of the Holy Spirit. He neither recognizes the difference between such divine grace and human kindness, nor that prayer is the spring from which it flows. He is the best pastor he can humanly be, but he fails to see that Christ Himself longs to shepherd the people, but will only do so as he the human pastor, hides in the shadow of constant, deliberate, prayerful dependence.

> Prayer is the life and soul of the sacred function; without it, we can expect no success in our ministry; without it, our best instructions are barren and our most painful labors idle. Before we can strike terror into those who break the law, we must first, like Moses, spend much time with God in retirement; prayer often gains a success to little talents, while the greatest without it are useless or pernicious. A minister who is not a man of piety and prayer, whatever his other talents may be, cannot be called a servant of God, but rather a servant of Satan, chosen by him for the same reason that he chose the serpent of old, because he was more subtle than any beast of the field which the Lord God had made. What a monster, oh God, must that minister of religion be, that dispenser of the ordinances of the gospel, that intercessor between God and His people, that reconciler of man to his Maker, if he sees himself not as a man of prayer.[11]

God blesses the people as the pastor prays for them. Pastors get the privilege of bringing the flock and their needs before the Lord, noting their needs, lamenting for their sin, praying for their growth and development, weeping for their lost sons and daughters. He stands in the gap for them. There is no way to measure what did not happen as a result of the shepherd's investment in watchful prayer. As a pastor calls up a name before God, out of the power of his office, it is as if he were, as a shepherd, laying that lamb in the arms of the Great Shepherd, placing it on some altar, imploring God for His hand to be on it, as a blessing. Others can pray for you and me, but a pastor has a special calling and office for such a task – he is the shepherd.

In the liturgical church, confidence is placed in the power of the *office* and the *rite*. In Pentecostal churches, confidence is placed in the *person* that seems to carry a special *anointing*. For evangelical non-Pentecostal churches, it is placed in neither. Rather, it is placed in *the Bible, the Word*. In truth, it is found in all of these – the office and the symbolic rites prescribed by Scripture, the special empowerment of the specific person, and the Word of God, often as a *rhema*.

In recent years, the role of the clergy has been re-fashioned as that of a professional. It is an attempt to regain cultural acceptance in the wake of the growing social hostility toward Christianity. But the approach is fatally flawed. Clergy should be professional in all they do, qualified and quality-oriented, skilled and trained, well-equipped and prepared to interact with professionals from any field. But ministry can never be a mere career path. It is a calling. It is divine service. One is captive to the will of God, and willingly so. And such service demands a relationship with God. The pastor must be, above all else, a holy man of God, and that is demonstrated by a life of prayer.

Why Pastors Should Pray

1. Prayer is the first duty of spiritual leaders. Paul, writing to the Romans, declares, *"God is my witness, whom I serve with my spirit in the Gospel of His Son, that without ceasing, I make mention of you always in my prayers"* (1:9). Prayer is the first of his divinely given duties mentioned. It is the greatest thing a pastor can do for his people.

2. Prayer is the mark of a leader's life. When Saul (Paul) was converted, the first sign of his changed heart was that he prayed differently (Acts 9:11). He was a Jew, a dedicated Pharisee, obviously he prayed. But now something was different. When the angel announced his conversion to Ananias in coaching the reluctant laymen to go minister to this violent persecutor of believers, the convincing evidence of his changed heart was, *"Behold, he is praying."* Without prayer, there is scant evidence that we have become a Christian. Simultaneously, prayer is the spring out of which changed lives draw strength and are prepared for ministry.

3. Prayer reveals our uneasiness with the world. The new birth removes the blindness, and even a new Christian recognizes that this world lies in darkness. His discomfort with sin is a gift; a new consciousness is at work in him. His daily escape from this darkness is found in prayer. Prayer is a protest against the way the world is, and the absence of prayer, the lack of time when the heart is turned heavenward, is a sign of being too much at home here. The name of God is dishonored here, even in the Church. The laws of God are broken, His kingdom is rejected. His Son is crucified, as it were, over and over, day after day. The uneasiness of our hearts and the condition of the world should crescendo into prayerful pleas for God to act, *"Will you not revive us again that your people may rejoice in you?"* (Psa. 85:6). There is an escalating urgency in a true believer, *"It is time for you to act, O Lord; for your law is being broken"* (Psa. 119:126). Living in a world, and even a church, that denies God's authority and resists His sovereignty, prayer is a plea for divine action.

4. Prayerlessness is at the root of ministry failures. When Jesus descended from the Mount of Transfiguration, He was confronted by a man

> *...falling on his knees before Him and saying, 'Lord, have mercy on my son, for he is a lunatic and is very ill; for he often falls into the fire and often into the water. I brought him to your disciples, and they could not cure him.' And Jesus answered and said, 'You unbelieving and perverted generation, how long shall I be with you? How long shall I put up with you? Bring him here to Me.' And Jesus rebuked him, and the demon came out of him, and the boy was cured at once* (Mt. 17:14-21).

The story is astounding and very humiliating for the disciples.

This is a strong rebuke. Jesus placed their blame on the failure of faith and prayer,

> *Because of the littleness of your faith…if you have faith the size of a mustard seed, you will say to this mountain, 'Move from here to there,' and it will move; and nothing will be impossible to you. But this kind does not go out except by prayer and fasting* (v. 20-21).

There are some things we may be able to face without prayer, even if such a practice is unwise; but there are other moments that will clearly show us our deficit without prayer. Human wisdom and authority is not adequate. If we want to be more effective Christians, if we want more of the power of the Spirit in our lives, we will pray!

5. Prayer and evangelism are connected. When the priority of prayer was reinstated by the apostles in Acts 6, the effect was phenomenal, "*…the Word of God spread and the number of the disciples multiplied greatly in Jerusalem, and a great many of the priests were obedient to the faith*" (v. 7). The potency was not in their sweat over tables, not in their labors, but in their intercession. In Psalm 50:7-12, God makes it clear that He does not need our prayers. We are the needy ones. Prayerfulness is a simple, open, honest declaration before God of total helplessness. If the work of God is to move forward, if people are to be convicted of sin and convinced of righteousness, if salvations are to abound, if the church is to grow in the grace and might of the Lord – it will be by our utter and absolute dependence on God demonstrated by prayer. God does not work because of who we are and what we are capable of, but in spite of it all. Pride is the stealth-like monster, the tasteless poison that always threatens us. And its medicine is humble prayer.

6. Prayer seizes kairos moments. Our roles, by Divine design, are often pivotal, potentially critical. God, indeed, positions us for *kairos* moments. Mordecai offered such an insight to Queen Esther, "*Who knows that you are come to the kingdom for such a time as this?*" (Esther 4:14). She was blind to fact that God's hand had positioned her, and it was urgent for her to act. The future of the Jewish people was in the balance; few national crises could surpass the urgency of this one. Still, she was reluctant, self-protecting, thinking in narrow self-interested ways. Her reluctance almost caused her to miss her destiny. Mordecai warned, *"Have you ever considered, Esther, that you are not indispensable? If you do nothing about it, deliverance will arise from another quarter."* (Esther 4:14). Our roles in kingdom purposes are at times heroic, grand and imposing. Rarely are we aware of the momentous power of such moments. But God is never without alternatives. *"Perhaps you have come to the Kingdom for such a time as this? Why not rise to the occasion rather than lose out?"* (Esther 4:14). God is sovereign. He has a plan. That plan will continue. He will build His Church and the gates of hell will not prevail against her. And yet, our participation in God's plan is tied to our obedience, and nowhere is that exemplified more clearly than our reporting for duty daily in prayer. Whether or not, and the degree to which we then participate in God's plan, is somehow rooted in prayer.

7. Prayer must move beyond experience to relationship. Prayer can never be a daily event or an episode. It is, at one level, of course, very daily and also an experience. But the purpose of specific daily time with God is that it becomes the portal through which we enter communion with God. David prayed seven times a day. Daniel, three times a day. As stated earlier, meeting a friend in the street, Wesley would say, "Brother, do I find you praying?" The Bible is full of recorded prayer moments and rich in prayer content. The psalms are the most obvious collection. And these prayers give us prayer models. They help us jump-start our own prayer lives. They provide language for prayer. The best praying involves praying Scripture!

8. Prayer demands faith. Faith rises out of God's Word; its certainty is made firm by the conviction that what we request is the will of God. Faith sees with the eyes of vision – God's vision for a matter or a person, a place or a time. Faith enforces the Lord's will. It calls things that are not as if they were. Luther boldly asserted, "Father, I will have my will because I know that my will is Your will." Prayer involves the attempt to discover God's will in a matter and then relentlessly persist until the answer comes. This is not attempting to persuade a reluctant God, but enforcing His will, arguing His rights and initiatives in the courtroom of heaven. The widow of Luke 18 persisted in prayer before the unjust judge, and Jesus reflected, *"Men ought always to pray and not lose heart"* (Luke 18:1). We appeal to the Judge of the earth, to God Himself, in His heavenly courtroom, and we ask for relief from our adversary, the devil. God's ruling in our behalf, the action of the court, His intervention and the victory that heaven's court enforces on the earth, if only for this matter or that, in this region and season of time, is, nevertheless, the signal that we are not widows. Answers to prayer, in the name of Jesus, to God as Father, are evidence that we are the authorized, legitimate bride of Christ, left with authority to finish His work.

9. Prayers need to be big! They need to be God-sized. We too often pray narrow, self-interested prayers. *"Ask of Me, and I will give You the heathen [the nations] for an inheritance,"* says the Father to the Son (Psa. 2:8). Think big when you pray!

10. Prayer exalts the name of the Lord. Finally, the ultimate goal of prayer is the exaltation of the name of God for the glory of God, *"Hallowed be your name"* (Mt. 6:9). The colonial preacher George Whitefield would say, "Let the name of George Whitefield perish, but let the name of Christ live on and on forever!" When Jesus Himself lifted up His eyes to heaven, He said, *"Father, the hour has come, glorify Your Son that Your Son also may glorify You. And now, O Father, glorify Me together with Yourself, with the glory which I had with You before the world was"* (John 17:5). The believer responds immediately with a hearty, "So be it." It is possible for the noblest motives to be skewed. We want to see men saved, particularly our loved ones, that they will not be lost forever, that we will enjoy their company in heaven. Such reasoning sounds noble, but salvation is not merely for our pleasure; that is a by-product. Salvation of souls is for the glory of God.

Gardiner Spring once observed:

> The time was when the pastors of the American churches valued the privilege of prayer; they were not only men of prayer, but they prayed often for and with one another. Their reciprocal and fraternal visits were consecrated and sweetened by prayer, nor was it any unusual thing for them to employ days of fasting and prayer together for the effusions of God's Spirit upon themselves and their churches, and they were days of power, days when God's arm was made bare and His right hand plucked out of His bosom, nor was it difficult to see then wherein the great strength of the pulpit lies. He that is feeble among them shall be as David, and the House of David shall be as God.[12]

Zechariah 8:20 predicts the day when,

> *Peoples shall yet come, even the inhabitants of many cities; the inhabitants of one city shall go to another saying, 'Let us go at once to entreat the favor of the Lord, and to seek the Lord of hosts; I am going.' Many peoples and strong nations shall come to seek the Lord of hosts in Jerusalem, and to entreat the favor of the Lord.*

Would we not want to see this in our day?

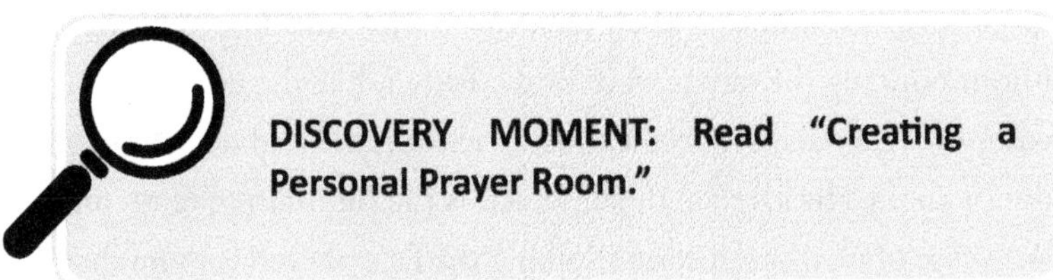
DISCOVERY MOMENT: Read "Creating a Personal Prayer Room."

Face Time with the Father

Increasingly, the culture grows more and more impersonal. Do such changes affect us? Technology allows for electronic connections;

global committee meetings via Skype and video conferencing are common. Holograms promise the day when people in different locations will appear to sit at the same conference table as three-dimensional images. They will appear to be present, but will actually be on the other side of the globe, their presence only simulated, only projected. Still, while some 59 percent see the positive contribution of electronic meetings, almost 80 percent prefer old-fashioned 'face time' meetings.[13] Some things must not change! To see prayer as replaceable, as old fashioned, as antiquated, is to attempt to replace God Himself.

In 1978, pediatric researchers discovered that an infant languishes without face-to-face encounters, in fact, without enlivened facial expressions. Innately, something deep in the infant resonates with a smile, the bright eyes and the radiant face placed close to their own. A consistent unresponsive face produces a wariness in the infant, followed by emotional withdrawal. The researchers called the impact significant.[14] The enlivened face of our Father is perhaps the most critical component of our prayer time. The priestly blessing included the line, *"May his face shine upon you!"* (Num. 6:24-26). Blessing, grace and peace were linked to God's countenance. Christians who have not learned that the 'face of God' lights up in their own don't know the value of personal time with God. Blessing and His smiling face go together, and it is likely that those who rush into their days without noticing the radiant face of the Father, like the infant are increasingly weary and register a sense of withdrawal and detachment, a doubt about His love for them, which is the fountain of faith, and a lost sense of vital connection. Seeking the face of God is more than a mere phrase.

---

1 This material is adapted from an article on John Welch, taken from John Howie's *Scots Worthies,* (1775; revised and enlarged, 1781). The original edition, W. H. Carslaw (Edinburgh: Johnstone: Hunter and Company, 1870), 118-

139. See: www.path2prayer.com/article/1137/revival-and-holy-spirit/books-sermons/new-resources/famous-christians-books-and-sermons/john-welch-mighy-man-of-prayer.

2 Leonard Ravenhill, *Why Revival Tarries* (Grand Rapids, MI: Bethany House, 1959, 1987), 15.

3 Daniel Henderson, *Transforming Prayer* (Minneapolis, MN: Bethany House, 2011), 40.

4 Ellison Research is a marketing research company in Phoenix. The sample of 868 Protestant ministers included only those who were actively leading churches. The study's total sample is accurate to within plus or minus 3.2 percentage points. The study was conducted in all 50 states, using a representative sample of pastors from all Protestant denominations. Respondents' geography, church size and denomination were tracked to ensure appropriate representation and accuracy. www.bpnews.net/bpnews.asp?ID=20918.

5 I am indebted to Martin Holdt and his article, "Intercessory Prayer: The Minister's Duty" for much of what follows in this next section, particularly the rationales for a praying pastor. The article can be seen in its entirety and original form at the website sponsored by 'Founders Ministries,' located at PO Box 150931, Cape Coral, FL 33915; (239) 772-1400. See: www.founders.org/journal/fj12/article3.html. Mr. Martin Holdt is the pastor of the Emmanuel Baptist Church in Johannesburg, South Africa. He is also the editor of Reformation Africa South.

6 Pew Public Forum, "Public Esteem for Military Still High" (Date of the Poll: July 11, 2013). www.pewforum.org/Other-Demographics/Public-Esteem-for-Military-Still-High.aspx.

7 E. M. Bounds, *Classic Collection on Prayer* (Alachua, FL: Bridge-Logos, 2001), 7.

8 This compilation of the brief profiles of great men of prayer was put together originally by Greg Gordon, founder of sermonindex.net ministry, and adapted for inclusion here.

9 Ravenhill.

10 Timothy Z. Witmer, *The Shepherd Leader at Home* (Wheaton, IL: Crossway, 2012), 17.

11 John Smith, *Lectures on the Nature and End of the Sacred Office* (Baltimore, MD: A. Neal, 1810), 32.

12 Martin Holdt, "Intercessory Prayer: The Minister's Duty," See: www.founders.org/journal/fj12/article3.html.

13 Daniel Henderson, *Transforming Prayer*, 34.

14 Ibid, 52.

15 Dallas Williard, quoted by James. C. Wilhoit, *Spiritual Formation as if the Church Mattered: Growing in Christ through Community* (Grand Rapids, MI: Baker Academic, 2008), 9.

16 Ibid.

17 James. C. Wilhoit, *Spiritual Formation as if the Church Mattered: Growing in Christ through Community* (Grand Rapids, MI: Baker Academic, 2008), 39.

18 Jim Thompson, *Positive Coaching: Building Character and Self-Esteem through Sports* (Portola Valley, CA; Warde Publishers, 1995), 69.

GROUP TALK

1. How much time do you want to spend in prayer daily, apart from ministry moments?
2. Do the great prayer legacies inspire you or condemn?
3. How can you use the model of prayer in the lives of these great saints to motivate you?
4. Whose prayer life strikes you as a compelling example?
5. Identify three things about them and their prayer life that inspire you.
6. Rehearse the section – the pastor as shepherd – and particularly focus on prayer and watching. Reflect on whether or not your life and practice is congruent with these ideas.
7. In this chapter, there are ten assertions about prayer. Rate these in terms, first of belief – do you agree or disagree? – and then, in terms of behavior. Note the incongruence between beliefs you affirm and behaviors you practice. Identify three areas for growth.

ACTION STEPS

1. Complete the rating sheet on the Ten Assertions of Prayer.
2. Rate these in terms of belief. Do you agree or disagree?
3. Then, rate them in terms of behavior. Do you practice these or not?
4. Finally, look for the items where you agree with the statement, but your behavior is not consistent with your beliefs.
5. Mark three areas for personal growth.

MILESTONE THREE

Things you should have in place now!

1. Your weekly **PRAYER MEETING** should be continuing. Stay at it. Don't give up!

2. You should be meeting monthly with potential **PRAYER LEADERS.** Your meetings may be like your early prayer gatherings – they start and stop. Some folks come and go. Here with potential leaders, as with your prayer meeting, be persistent. You are not looking for the fast horses out of the gate, but for those who keep pace in the backstretch. You are still not ready to 'go public' with the new prayer initiative.

   You want a stable core at your prayer gatherings and a sense of momentum (moving toward the 20% mark) before you go public. And you want a stable core at your prayer leadership gatherings (moving toward the 3-5% mark).

3. **The PERSONAL PRAYER Life Challenge.** The last of the three legs of our stool is really the first – and that is your own daily personal prayer habit. Here is why we listed it last. You cannot wait until you have achieved some perfect personal prayer plateau. And often, you will find the motivation to meet God personally when you meet God regularly with others. Left to yourself, and with the other elements of the prayer initiative subordinated to personal prayer, you might delay action. But if you begin with public prayer, and 'hem yourself in' by meeting regularly with your prayer learning-leaders, you are more likely to overcome the stop-start pattern of personal prayer.

   Make no mistake. Public prayer without the development of this private counterpart will leave your prayer effort handicapped. It needs a leader who meets with God, hears from God and longs to obey God by grace. Your prayer effort needs leaders who pray.

THESE THREE INDESPENSABLE, CORROLARY ACTIONS ARE FOUNDATIONAL. If necessary, do these and worry about nothing else! You may start and stop, spit and sputter. Don't give up! Establishing a praying church will be the hardest task you tackle! And it will also be the most rewarding and fruitful.

If you do NOTHING MORE than continue to weave these three strands of prayer together – personal, the corporate (the church gathered in prayer), and quietly developing potential prayer leaders – you will succeed in your prayer ministry.

BEYOND THE THREE SIMPLE STEPS

CHAPTER 8
Long Term Process

At West Point, there is a saying, "No plan survives contact with the enemy."[1] Unpredictable things happen outside your control. The army has a crisp, plain-talk statement stamped on all its orders – called a CI. That is code for the Commander's Intent. It is a reminder not to get lost in the details of a battle plan and lose the war. It is permission to improvise, on the spot, as long as the ultimate objective is in mind. The details, the *tactical* steps, are subordinate to the overall *strategy*, and the strategic plan itself has its roots in the *mission* and *vision*. Strategies and tactics change – the mission and vision, the *values* that drive them and inform them are constant. It is the core of the idea that is important.

PHASE I – Learning About and Doing Prayer – The Launch (3 Simple Processes)

Milestone One:[2] Launch a Church-wide Prayer Meeting

As a pastor, lead the people into prayer. This is one area the pastor cannot delegate. You can only lead people where you yourself go. You may find someone you can share leadership with, but you will need to model prayer, and you will need to call the group to prayer. They need to see and hear you pray.

Don't worry about the attendance. Pray, even if no one shows up. This is not a meeting *with people,* it is a meeting *for* people *with God.* Persist in prayer.

Limit the meeting to sixty to ninety minutes. Start on time and stop on time. Your people will appreciate your exercise of discipline. If there appears to be an unusual stirring of the Spirit, acknowledge it, release those who have to go with your blessing, and allow others to tarry. The noon-time prayer meetings that sparked the 3rd Great Awakening were punctual in their start and finish and yet, one million came to Christ.

Direct the prayer experience without quenching the Spirit. The ideal is a corporate prayer experience, not merely individual prayer experiences in a corporate setting. You want, at points, to focus prayer, to get the group on the same page. Use a variety of prayer methods and models, yet within a single framework. Find what works for you, then settle into the balance of predictability and flexibility. Introduce new prayer styles, but be sensitive to the wineskins you are pouring into. Generally, adapt the elements of Paul's theology of prayer – thanksgiving and praise; worshipful communion with God (pray the Bible); intercession (for

> First, start a Prayer Meeting! You are not praying unless you are meeting to pray. You must pray from the office of the Church; personal prayer cannot take the place of corporate prayer. Every church needs a worship-word service, a training-education-discipleship meeting, AND A PRAYER MEETING.

the lost, the unreached, etc.); and then personal needs. Remember the warning of Jesus – when fervency invades rigidity, there is a total loss! The relational structure is damaged and the cause is lost. Don't quench the Spirit, yet, you must temper change. Your goal is the measured, tempered integration of prayer into the fabric of both the life of the congregation and families.

Erroll Hulse says, "The weekly prayer meeting is the spiritual barometer for any local church."[3] The language of prayer reveals the soul-health of the church. Are the prayers consumed with self – 'prayer requests'? Are there regular tears for the lost? Do the people pray with a Bible in their hand? Do they claim the promises? Is the Spirit evident in the midst of the prayer meeting? Are prayers being answered? Is there any attempt to discern the will of God, to see the hand of God?

DISCOVERY MOMENT: Review "Just a Prayer Meeting."

The content and focus of the prayers reveals the spiritual health and vitality of the people. Dead, self-interested praying evidences flesh-bound hearts. Passionate prayers that believe urge God's action according to Scripture. They promise our obedience and evidence faith. Heartfelt, tender prayers with wet eyes are evidence of a hunger for God, and often, a desire to see others come to Christ. If there are intercessors present who carry an assignment to pray for revival, for the nation, for the Great Commission, it will be evident. World events and needs will press in on the prayer time. Prayer meetings reveal what one cannot see on Sunday morning when everyone is neatly packed in rows and navigating together through the litany of worship. In prayer meetings, the desires of the heart are unpacked and revealing declarations are made public through prayer. We pray about what we care about. The church prayer meeting either reveals a caring congregation that feels the pain of the lost around them or has become oblivious to any concerns but those in our narrow world.

Consider the subjects that cry out for intercession: family concerns and anxieties, church issues, the passing needs for ongoing evangelism, regional and national concerns, the world of missions, missionaries, the global situation with the agony of regional civil war, drought, famine, or extreme poverty, the desperate need for stable government and rulers of integrity (1 Tim 2:1-4).

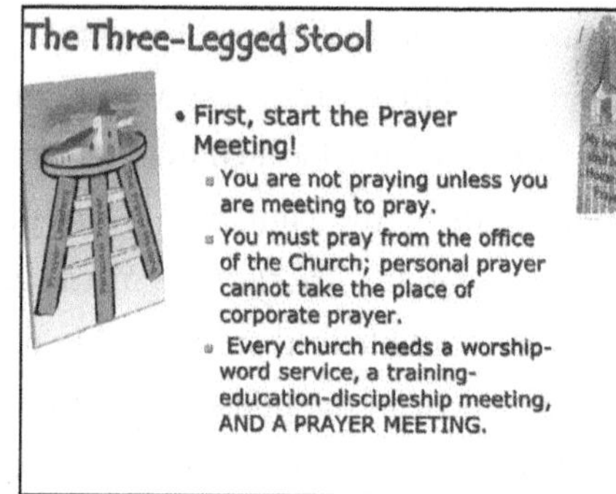

The Three-Legged Stool
• First, start the Prayer Meeting!
You are not praying unless you are meeting to pray.
You must pray from the office of the Church; personal prayer cannot take the place of corporate prayer.
Every church needs a worship-word service, a training-education-discipleship meeting, AND A PRAYER MEETING.

At times, you may want to open the church for daily prayer. In many parts of the world, Korea and Indonesia, for example, one of the features of church life is the proliferation of daily, early-morning prayer meetings. These have become a staple of church life, a lifestyle across denominational lines. In 1866, Spurgeon instituted daily prayer meetings at the Tabernacle. They were held twice daily, at 7 a.m. and 7:30 p.m. One main weekly prayer meeting took place on Monday evenings and was led by Pastor Spurgeon and attended by some 3,000 people, more than half of his Sunday morning attendance. (Note: See the recommendations in Special Days of Prayer and how to Plan a Prayer Meeting. Those ideas will help you in your weekly prayer gathering as well.)

Milestone Two: Develop a Prayer Leadership-Learning Team

This is not your typical small group! You are drawing around you folks who might catch from you a passion for the Lord, a desire to pray, and an increased capacity to encourage others to spend time with God.

What follows does not sound 'simple.' Read through it carefully and then read the synopsis. As you meet with your small group of potential prayer leaders, remember the following:

- The most important element is **relational.**
- The second is a learned **appreciation for the value of prayer** – and at the heart of that value is a celebration of God's love and a developing passion for Him. Short and simple. You want to create a group who will 'catch' your passion for the Lord!

The Three-Legged Stool

- Second, look for teachable, potential prayer leaders.
  - Don't appoint prayer leaders, call together prayer learners!
  - If prayer leaders are not humble enough to learn, if they are stuck in styles of prayer that confine them, in a prayer culture that is narrow – your effort will be stymied at best or perhaps completely fail.
  - Cultivate an openness to prayer styles, a more holistic understanding of prayer and a healthy team dynamic.

- The third element is the invisible glue of grace that flows in the room. It is a **cultivated respect – the *ethos*** that we have spoken of, the kind of atmosphere and relational health that you would like to characterize the entire church. This intangible will hardly be recognized by most. It is like the wallpaper, like the air we breathe – it is mostly noticeable in its toxic absence. "'Lot of tension in the room tonight, honey, wasn't there?'... 'I don't think they like one another very much!'...'Wonder what she was so stressed about?'...'They seemed very uncomfortable praying aloud, didn't they?'... 'Can you believe what he did/what they said?'" Pride and conflict appear like

> In the planning stage, you must *"Shrink the change."* Make the change small, incremental, and increase the possibility of success. In shrinking the change, and granting a sense of success, you grow the people, build faith, change habits and rally the herd for the next challenge, preserving your unity and momentum.[6]

flashing lights and screaming sirens; humility and unity are more like a quiet, comforting stream, sadly, hardly noticed. As much as you want to get to content, the greater need is to cultivate culture – a prayer culture, a Christ-like culture, an open hunger to grow in Christ. You are reinterpreting Biblical Christianity for your people, moving away from a performance and content basis to that of humility and dependence on God, coupled with bold confidence and faith.

- The fourth element is **content.** You want to stretch the group's theology of prayer. You want to expand their prayer experiences. So, of course, a part of your time together is teaching/training. As you teach, you are looking for those who are most teachable. You will discover several different types of folks in the room. Superficial learners and profound learners – the latter group will take learning seriously and apply it to their lives. You will discover those who learn with their head and others who learn with their hearts. You will discover those who are ready learners, some because they have no prior learning about prayer or prayer models, theology or philosophy. Others will be 'resistant learners.' They may be struggling with prior learning about prayer; stretched, they are like someone trying to find a place for something that is both heavy and fragile. They don't have a ready mental slot for the idea; they need more time to process. Mark the profound heart learners who struggle to think through the material. (Learning Team Materials, Coaching, etc.)
- The fifth element is **the cultivation of discernment**. Do you have a group that, first of all, discerns truth – they begin to have 'aha' moments as you proceed to unwrap the theology of prayer and proceed with 'learning team' content? They make connections to pieces of truth they already possess. They deconstruct and reconstruct prayer ideas. They develop an ability to disagree agreeably. They state principles of truth in love. They hold to certain convictions but in a complimentary, non-contradictory, way. They see the value

of teaming. They discern one another's gifts; they add value to one another. A teaming culture develops.

- The sixth element is **leadership** and cultivating prayer leaders. Who in your group can teach the material to others? Who can lead or organize? Who will make a great partner to a leader/organizer? Who leads with grace? Who are the finishers? Finishers are folks who understand the principles but are not stage folks. They help you finish, close the ranks, stay together and drive the final nail in the project. They pick up the stragglers, move along the edge of the crowd and calm those who misunderstand or need a bit more personal attention. They are like shepherd leaders who bring up the rear. They keep people from falling through the cracks. They are great glue in a social group. They display genuine love to everyone.
- The seventh element is **vision and strategic planning.** Once a 'big picture' of prayer (vision) emerges, and you see the exploding possibilities of prayer ministry and how it relates to all the other aspects of ministry, you need a 'big picture plan' (strategy) that conceptualizes how the parts fit together and how they are unwrapped tactically. For example, do you start with prayer walking or with the mobilization of intercessors? Do you train in prayer basics or spiritual warfare? Values clarify vision. Vision (the big picture) needs strategy (a big picture plan) and strategy is unwrapped piece by piece (tactics). Each tactical component and its leader should know how the prayer cause they lead relates to others. For example, if we fail in getting men to pray, it is unlikely that we will succeed with the family altar! If we fail in training healthy intercessors and mobilizing them, our efforts in prayer evangelism will face great challenges.

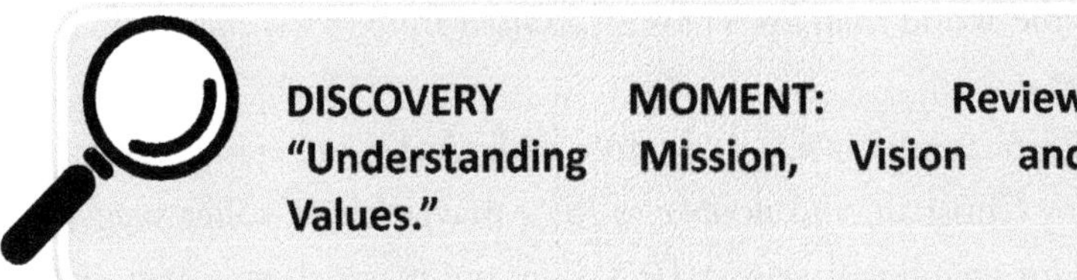

DISCOVERY MOMENT: Review "Understanding Mission, Vision and Values."

Depending on the size of your church, here are some leadership minimums:

Church Size	*Prayer Learning Team Size*
0-50	2-3
50-100	3-5
100-200	5-7
200-500	6-10
500-1,000	7-15
1,000	12 plus

SYNOPSIS: Convene a small group regularly to encourage a spirit of prayer in an atmosphere of love and mutual respect, where learning is appreciated and applied, and where leaders emerge who are capable of articulating vision, developing strategy, planning and executing various aspects of an expanding prayer effort.

Milestone Three: The Personal Prayer Life Challenge

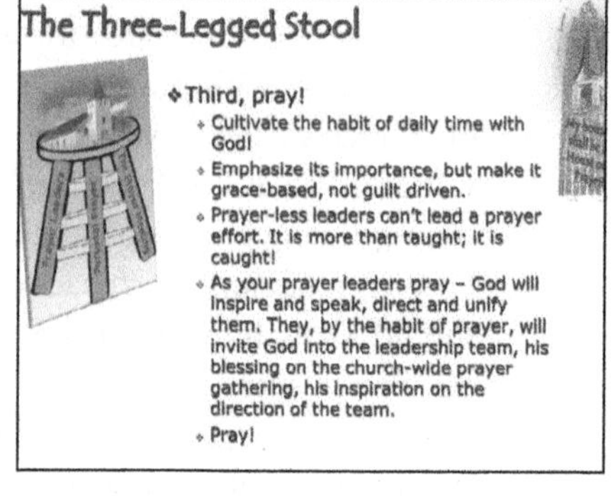

The Three-Legged Stool
Third, pray!
Cultivate the habit of daily time with God!
Emphasize its importance, but make it grace-based, not guilt driven.
Prayer-less leaders can't lead a prayer effort. It is more than taught; it is caught!
As your prayer leaders pray – God will inspire and speak, direct and unify them. They, by the habit of prayer, will invite God into the leadership team, his blessing on the church-wide prayer gathering, his inspiration on the direction of the team.
Pray!

Use resources as simple as the 'Our Daily Bread' prayer guide. Encourage a psalm-a-day. Encourage members to read it and then to pray it. Model scripture praying in your corporate prayer meeting. Pray the prayers of Paul. Print daily devotional ideas in your church bulletin. Introduce the World Map Prayer Guide. (Order from: www.ehc.org/free-prayer-maps.)

Emphasize that this **daily time with God** is imperative for any serious Christian, and doubly so for a prayer leader. Offer suggestions for spending time with God. Print out materials on a 'personal prayer retreat.' Teach about praying the Scriptures and offer models for private time with God. Do it consistently and gently. Relentlessly define Christianity as relational – it requires regular communion and intimacy with God.

> John Wooden, the great coach at UCLA, a believer said, "When you improve a little each day, eventually big things occur...Don't look for quick, big improvement. Seek the small improvement one day at a time. That's the only way it happens — and when it happens, it lasts." The power is in 'small visible goals' that build momentum.[7]

Do this in the weekly prayer meeting as well, gently – not driving, but leading; not a matter of law, but of grace – then challenge your leaders, and, finally, engage the congregation in a grace-based personal devotional life.

Jerry Kirk has introduced some great materials that encourage people to pray a simple prayer for themselves and others called the '40 Day Prayer Covenant.' This simple prayer plan is helpful in getting people to commit to pray. It gives them a track for prayer – many people struggle with knowing what and how to pray. This material can be found at theprayercovenant.org/the-prayer-covenant.

NOW

In order to both *LEARN AND DO Prayer*
You have a WEEKLY PRAYER MEETING,
DAILY TIME WITH GOD by Leaders, and
Your MONTHLY PRAYER LEADERS MEETING.

CHECK POINT!

Don't press any further until you sense that your prayer meeting is catching heaven's wind and fire; and, you have a small team of developing leaders who are learning and growing together with the promise of leading the congregation through significant prayer reformation; and they evidence a hunger for God as they meet with God daily, personally. Without learning leaders and a growing number of people attending your church-wide prayer meeting whose daily prayer habits evidence new vitality you can't move forward.

Your goal is not information about prayer, but spiritual formation in the presence of God in prayer; not merely the activity of prayer – but a transforming relationship with God, personally and congregationally. If this is happening – move forward; if not, something is missing in your recipe.

These three – a healthy congregational prayer meeting; humble, praying, learning leaders, and the promise of recovering the family altar out of a daily personal at-home prayer time – are critical foundation pieces.

PHASE II – Discovery

You now want to enter into a research-discovery phase. You don't want to guess about the depth and level of personal and congregational prayer – you want factual data. You also want facts about the challenges of reaching the harvest around you. You will move through three sequential milestones in this phase.

1. Extensive discovery and research. This will demand that you enlarge your team.
2. You will conduct a planning retreat, adding additional congregational members and leaders, reviewing the data from your research and projecting a plan for prayer engagement.
3. You will confirm a core prayer leadership team.

MILESTONE FOUR

Things you should have in place now!

1. The congregation has a **PRAYER MEETING**
2. There is a small group of developing **PRAYER-LEARNING LEADERS.**
3. You are engaging in regular **PERSONAL PRAYER.**

YOU ARE...

Doing Prayer – Personally and Corporately

And you are Learning and Leading

Your Three-legged Stool:

Three simple but powerful actions!

4. **Discovery**

Milestone Four: Research and Discovery

You are now ready to enter a research-discovery stage. You will need to lay assumptions aside.

- You are going to look INSIDE your congregation to discover the degree to which members are engaged in prayer. How much are they praying and about what?
- You are going to look BACK. What is the history of prayer in the congregation? Are there people who can tell stories of your church as a praying congregation?
- Look AROUND to discover other praying churches and learn from them.
- Then look OUT at the harvest field around you and the needs. Prayer cannot be focused inwardly. It must have a missional, prayer-evangelism dimension. Define your harvest field around your church location and in the city-county.

Twenty Indicators of a Spiritual Awakening

"What would a contemporary spiritual awakening look like in America...in our church and culture?" Prayer leader Bob Bakke says, "There are 20 indicators that will signal a Great Awakening in America: 10 in the Church and 10 in the Culture. These spiritual indicators will ignite a passion for the body of Christ to unify in prayer, as we prepare our states, our counties, and our hearts."

Consider these in your research. Use the accompanying rating sheet in *Perspectives*. Are there indicators in your church of a spiritual awakening? In the culture of your city?

IN THE CHURCH

1. Increasing testimony of the manifest Presence of God
2. Increased conversions and baptisms
3. Amplified participation in corporate as well as individual prayer, fasting, and other spiritual disciplines leading to more effective discipleship
4. A decrease in divorces and renewed commitment to marriage between a man and a woman in covenant relationship as God intends
5. Imparting faith to children and youth as parents are equipped by the church to become primary disciplers of their children
6. Among churches, a passionate pursuit for the well-being of their cities through the planting of new congregations, benevolent ministries, practical service and focused evangelism
7. Commitment to radical generosity as evidenced by compassion ministries and global missions
8. Improved health among ministers as evidenced by their joy, decreased resignations, healthy loving relationships within their families, and an increased response among young people called to the ministry
9. Christians involved in bold witness accompanied by

miracles, dramatic conversions and Holy Spirit empowered victories over evil

10. Heightened expressions of love and unity among all believers, as demonstrated by the unity of pastors and leaders

AWAKENING INDICATORS IN THE CULTURE

1. Breakdowns of racial, social and status barriers as Christ's church celebrates together – Jesus!
2. A restoration of morality, ethical foundations and accountability among leaders of church and government, business and politics
3. A transformation of society through the restoration of Christ's influence in the arts, media, and communication
4. Increased care for the hungry and homeless, the most vulnerable and needy
5. Young adults, students and children embracing the claims and lifestyle of Christ through the witness of peers who live and love as Jesus
6. Community and national leaders seeking out the church as an answer to society's problems
7. Increased care for children as "gifts from the Lord" as the gospel addresses abortion, adoption, foster care and child well-being
8. Righteous relations between men and women: decrease in divorce rates, co-habitation, same-sex relations, sexual abuse, sexual trafficking, out of wedlock children and STDs
9. An awakening to the "fear of the Lord" rather than the approval of people, thus restoring integrity and credibility
10. Neighborhood transformation and an accompanying decrease of social ills through increased expressions of "loving your neighbor" in service, compassion and unity

ACTION STEP: Complete the Rating Sheet: Twenty Indicators of a Spiritual Awakening.

- Finally, look UP. From the start, let God set the pace. Be dependent on Him. Let Him lead. Keep your eyes heavenward.

To accomplish this research, you will need to add members to your learning team without diluting the culture of the team. Note: you will find additional help for your research in the book: *Milestones – Markers on the Journey to become a House of Prayer* and *Transforming Your Church into a House of Prayer – Revised Edition.*

MILESTONE FIVE

Things you should have in place now!

1. The congregation has a **PRAYER MEETING**
2. There is a small group of developing **PRAYER-LEARNING LEADERS.**
3. You are engaging in regular **PERSONAL PRAYER.**

YOU ARE...

Doing Prayer – Personally and Corporately

And you are Learning and Leading

Your Three-legged Stool:

Three simple but powerful actions!

4. **RESEARCH AND DISCOVERY**
5. **PLANNING**

Milestone Five: Planning –

Articulating Vision and Mission, Strategy and Tactics

Now, using your research, set forth an informed plan. Your goal is to raise the level of prayer in your congregation, in all four dimensions – at-home praying; at-church praying; mobilized and directed intercessory prayer; and prayer evangelism. This will rekindle revival fires. You want to implement best prayer practices discovered from other congregations. You want to engage the congregation to not only pray for internal needs, but also to focus on the harvest and see the church as a community transformational force – all without losing prayer's heart, which is congregational exposure to God's loving and holy Presence.

For this milestone, a leadership planning retreat is recommended. Use *Transforming Your Church into a House of Prayer* as a guide.

The key participants – your learning-leaders, your discovery team (members who helped you with research) and congregational leaders (staff, elders, deacons, department/ministry leaders, etc.) – need to be at this retreat.

Come out of the retreat with at least a sketched plan for the next three-to-five years. Hammer out your prayer values, the purpose of your prayer effort, a strategy. Develop a vision statement. Vision describes what-we-will-look-like-when-we-get there. It is the mountain your congregation must climb to meet with God in order to change the world. Remember, vision and mission statements sometimes get revised – it's the hammering them out, the agreement on core values and purpose, strategy and the next steps that is important.

Milestone Six: Affiirming Leaders (Leadership Structuring and Affirmation)

You might have been tempted to take the step of appointing leaders earlier – most processes would have already confirmed leaders. In prayer, hierarchical leadership is less important than example, humility and peer unity of heart and purpose. In the context of prayer, leaders often emerge. Starting with a small learning-leader team, you have added others twice – first, to assist with research; and then, at your planning retreat. With an informed plan, you will now move from learning by experience and exposure, to leading. You now need to restructure your core leaders, affirm and empower them to move forward. They have prayed together, learned together, explored and planned together – now, they must boldly, but humbly lead.

> Successful people don't passively ride out a difficult transition. They don't opt to merely survive it. Rather, they lean into it. They push harder. They change the rules of change.[8]

In smaller churches, you probably want a team of at least three-five core prayer leaders, perhaps more. Eventually, each of these may take on specific aspects of your prayer effort, so keep that in mind. Around this core, you have a larger team that helped with research and has also prayed and learned together. You will need to keep engaging them as well. Don't be surprised if one or more end up on your core team. If so, be sure to revisit the things they may have missed in the earlier training.

YOU HAVE COMPLETED RESEARCH, PROJECTED A PLAN AND AFFIRMED YOUR LEARNING TEAM AS A LEADERSHIP TEAM.

Think about the prayer ministry of your church in layers.

Even the prayer life of Jesus had multiple dimensions. He prayed alone. He prayed with His disciples. He went to the synagogue where the people gathered to pray, and to the temple as well. He prayed in public and in private, in sacred and secular places, with and for others. In the history of the early church, we find private prayer, prayer in groups, and the practice of going to the temple for prayer, personal connections with others in prayer.

"A three-fold cord," the Bible says, *"is not quickly broken!"*

The church-wide prayer meeting is the driving force in all the prayer activities. It feeds all the remainder. But the different layers mean a much more diverse prayer effort.

The Layers of Prayer

Adopt a mission field near and far

Engage Intercessors/Team them/Direct

Prayer Group Ministry

Frequent Morning/Evening Prayer Options

Prayer Sunday School Class/Teaching/Training

Engage Men/Women in Prayer

CHURCH PRAYER MEETING

DAILY, AT-HOME, PERSONAL PRAYER

Nurture Personal/Family Prayer

Church Departments: Youth/Children's/Senior

Prayer Evangelism/Mission Options

Relational Prayer Experiences (Circle of Prayer)

Specialized Prayer Meetings: Healing Teams/
Altar Teams/Outreach Prayer

Create a Prayer Room/Prayer Wall/Place and Space

DISCOVERY MOMENT: Watch the video "Developing Layers of Prayer."

YOU ARE NOW READY TO ENGAGE THE CONGREGATION IN A MUCH BROADER CALL TO PRAYER.

For the moment, you are only introducing prayer experiences, doorways that might lead to the development of these layers. A single prayer thread is inadequate for the spiritual stress you are facing, even now, not to speak of increased spiritual adversity if you begin, by prayer and evangelism, to impact the darkness. Single threads (intercessors and people of prayer) woven together become strands, and strands woven together become the strong rope capable of tethering a ship in a storm.

You want to build a prayer rope! Multiple strands and streams of prayer, layers of prayer.

The more of these streams and threads of prayer that flow and wind through your church and the families of the church, the more likely prayer will survive. Start multiple streams. Affirm mature leaders. Hand off the leadership of a new prayer effort, and yet, bind that prayer effort to the whole; make that leader a part of the church-wide prayer council.

Don't go forward, if you have not set forth an 'informed plan' out of significant research. Accurate information is fuel for intercession. You need the jolting awareness of what you are facing, the challenge of the harvest. The congregation must 'see the harvest' in order to 'pray to the Lord of the harvest' with greater passion. It must sense its own prayerlessness and the depth of tearless praying and lack of appropriate concern for God's missional agenda. Only with 'informed leaders' and a compelling plan out of sound data should you move forward.

PHASE III – GOING PUBLIC: FEEDING THE PRAYER FIRE AND FINDING LEADERS

Milestone Seven: Envisioning the Congregation

It is not that you have been keeping your prayer effort altogether a secret – rather, you have been building quietly and deeply. You have been mentoring a small group of potential prayer leaders, and calling aside members of your congregation to test their interest in prayer. With them, you have been cultivating hearts of prayer realizing that it is often easier to change the culture of a small group than that of the entire congregation. Change is incremental – and you know, if you persist and you are successful, the small group will influence the congregation. In the beginning, you probably realized that both you as a pastor and the people lack the private prayer roots necessary to lead a congregation in prayer. Public prayer efforts require private prayer practices. We have, in our age, virtually abandoned deep dependence on God in prayer. You, and your leaders, needed time to develop your own personal prayer habit.

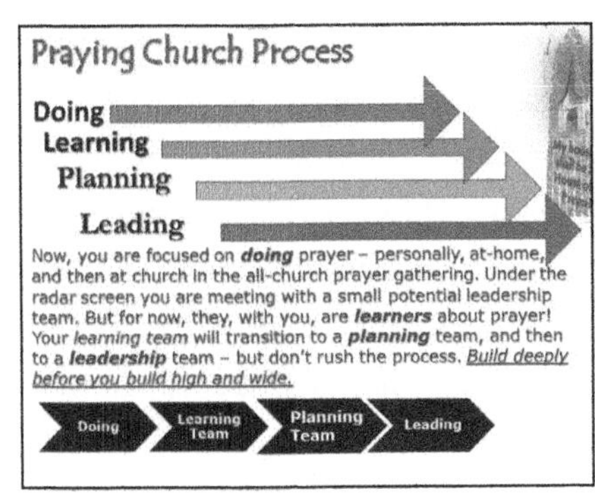

Then, you gathered data – to determine the depth and breadth of prayer in your congregation. You completed the other research regiments and collected the data in reports. You used that data to project a plan to move forward and empowered your core leadership team.

Now you are ready to envision the congregation to become a house of prayer for the nations. With an informed plan for moving forward, and committed, grounded leaders it is time to call the congregation to own the vision of becoming a house of prayer. You have invited them consistently to a congregational prayer meeting. Most, perhaps, have never come. You have been vetting and testing leaders, attempting to go deeper than wider – now, you are ready to go wide. (Learn more about an envisioning evening in *The Praying Church Resource Guide* available at www.alivepublications.org.)

Invite everyone to join you. Announce the evening well in advance. Choose your fellowship commons or some informal area. In a smaller church, this might even be held in someone's home. Make the folks comfortable. There is a suggested schedule in the *Praying Church Resource Guide.* However, the purpose is simple - talk about the importance of prayer and how the church should be a house of prayer for the nations. Share vision and plans. Have members of your core leadership team talk about their experience of meeting together and their research. Pray together.

Your bottom line is to test the level of interest in launching a prayer effort/ministry in your church. You want to cast vision for a broad-based prayer effort. Tell the stories of what is happening around the world in prayer. Inspire the idea of prayer in your congregation. Listen to hearts – and especially to the prayers people pray. Take time to have them share with one another in small groups. Record the insights. Compile a list of those present. Catalog ideas and note those who might be tapped to lead some aspect of your prayer effort. In this evening, you are not launching your prayer effort, you are envisioning. You are testing interest. Looking for potential leaders of the various aspects of prayer as you expand into the four dimensions. You are listening to hearts.

Poll the interest of the group in various prayer ministry areas (just an example):

1. Intercessory prayer.
2. Family prayer.
3. Church-based prayer groups.
4. Establishing a prayer room.

5. Integrating prayer into the ministries of the church.
6. Prayer training.
7. Youth/children's prayer.
8. Prayer evangelism.
9. Beginning prayer groups.
10. Establishing a pastor's prayer team.

From that meeting, enlarge your circle of potential prayer leaders. Do so based on the next milestone. Develop a plan to engage your congregation in prayer over the next year. Your core prayer leaders will certainly be involved, but this is also a chance to establish 'task teams' each with a prayer focus – personal prayer, family enrichment, intercessory prayer, prayer evangelism, prayer training. These task teams will evolve, around your core leaders, as the prayer leadership team for each of your focus areas, based on the Seven Markers of a Praying Church. You want this enlarging group to develop a teaming, praying culture. Keep the door open for new leaders. Keep inviting. Keep the 'movement' in the prayer effort.

Now you should be ready to add additional calls to prayer, frequently enough, to keep the call to prayer fresh before the entire congregation. On occasion, bring prayer 'front and center' to the Sunday service. Create on-ramps into the prayer process.

Project a year of prayer activities. See *The Praying Church Resource Guide* (order from www.alivepublications.org) for suggestions. Or go to www.projectpray.org. But remember, 'one' with God is a majority. While you *want* everyone involved and engaged in prayer, you don't *need* everyone to change the culture of the church – you only need 20% who are consistently committed to seeking God to join the prayer effort.

DISCOVERY MOMENT: Review the "Laws of Prayer Ministry."

Milestone Eight: Church-wide Enlistment

Gently and persistently, you now want to engage the congregation to embrace the practice of prayer. For the next year, offer an increasing variety of prayer challenges beyond your weekly prayer meeting – personal prayer, couples and family prayer, intercessory prayer and evangelism, prayer for the church, the nation and the world. Develop a calendar of prayer.

Keep it simple! Don't overload either your congregation or your learning-leader group! As you sense that the congregation is ready, and as you need more options to satisfy their growing hunger for prayer experiences, here are some additional ideas.

1. ***Special Days of Prayer*** – Host Special Days of Prayer, at least one per quarter. On those days, call the entire congregation to prayer. Create moments of prayer in the Sunday service. Host a special evening prayer service, Offer additional optional prayer activities on the weekend.

2. ***Virtual Prayer Meeting*** – Join other congregations in a 21-day virtual prayer experience each year in January. Millions of Americans are now fasting for some period of time in that month. Fasting is one of the key disciplines urged by Jesus. It controls all things internal. www.americapray.net

3. ***Seek God for the City*** – Join congregations across the nation in a prayer-evangelism experience in the traditional season of Lent, the 40 days leading up to Palm Sunday. This extraordinary guide takes the believer around the world. Every day, there is a slice of the city and a prayer walking suggestion. Across the nation, more than 100,000 Christians across denominational lines join the effort in conjunction with Waymakers. www.waymakers.org

4. ***National Day of Prayer*** – This is the only day sanctioned by Congress as a day of prayer for the nation. It is always the first Thursday in May. Have a prayer meeting. Join in a city-wide prayer meeting. If one is not planned, organize one. www.nationaldayofprayer.org

5. ***Global Day of Prayer*** – Around the world, millions pray on 'Pentecostal Sunday.' Join PCCNA churches for a prayer-care-share Pentecost Sunday emphasis in 2018, 2019 and 2020. www.globaldayofprayer.com

6. ***Call2Fall*** – Call2Fall is a moment of prayer sponsored by the Family Research Council that calls congregations across the nation to prayer on the Sunday before July 4th. www.call2fall.org

7. ***Patriot Day*** – September 11 has emerged as a special day of prayer in the United States. It is a day to 'cry out' for revival and awakening. The day is now resourced by the National Day of Prayer Committee.

8. ***30 Days of Prayer for the Muslim World*** – Coincides yearly with Ramadan, an important month of fasting and religious observance for Muslims. Christians worldwide are called upon to make an intentional but respectful effort during that period to learn about, pray for and reach out to Muslim neighbors. www.30daysprayer.com

9. ***Day of Prayer for the Peace of Jerusalem*** – On the first Sunday of every October, hundreds of millions of people around the world join together to pray for the peace of Jerusalem. In just a few years, this event has quickly become the largest Israel-focused prayer event in history. www.daytopray.com

10. ***10/40 Window Sunday*** – Praying Through the Window is a worldwide prayer initiative focused on a breakthrough in global terrorism and worldwide religions. 10/40 Window Sunday is a call to mobilize churches and individual prayer intercessors worldwide to intercede for these 68 nations. win1040.com

11. ***Global Prayer for Unreached People Groups*** – A challenge to the Global Church to collectively pray at least one billion prayer minutes for the unreached peoples of the world with a focus on the initiative on the last Sunday of October.
billion.tv/networking/prayer

12. ***International Days of Prayer for the Persecuted Church*** – Pray that in spite of the pressure and persecution, our suffering brothers and sisters – whereever they may be in the world — would stand firm in their faith, holding fast to the promises of God in Christ. First and Second Sunday of November. idop.org

Special days of prayer give you the opportunity to expose the entire church to prayer experiences, gradually integrating prayer into the culture of the Church. Consistently hosting special days of prayer introduces your prayer effort to Sunday morning attendees who may not yet participate in your weekly church-wide prayer meeting.

DISCOVERY MOMENT: Read "Planning Special Days of Prayer."

Phil Miglioratti, founder of the National Pastors Prayer Network and leader in the Mission America Coalition, gave this report:

> Nine years into my pastoring of a small, suburban congregation all heaven broke loose. On a Sunday in December, 1989, like the Berlin Wall that had recently crumbled half-way across the globe, a wall came crashing down in our church. Our creative but comfortable evangelical congregation suddenly went from singing three short choruses to worshipping for thirty minutes or more. Our theology of the Holy Spirit went from belief to experience. We began a journey that took us into realms of prayer we had never imagined.
>
> Over a decade later, I learned an important lesson as I reviewed our journey. I realized the Holy Spirit had led us into a *rhythm* of praying. The rhythm of our praying allowed all of us, not just individuals, to move closer to the Apostle Paul's command to "pray continually" (1 Thessalonians 5:17). Hardly realizing how it had happened, we had developed an approach to praying that was daily, weekly, monthly, seasonal, and annual.

With a variety of prayer opportunities, we involved more than just the praying core of the congregation in different forms of significant and strategic prayer.

Here is a sample of some of the things his congregation did as they developed a rhythmic pattern for prayer:

- *Daily* – My goal was for prayer to permeate the life of every member of our congregation every day. Sometimes I asked everyone to follow the same daily prayer guide such as *Seek God for the City* (www.waymakers.org) so that we all were praying toward the same needs or issues on the same day. Regularly, I reinforced the prayer habit in my sermons and teachings as well as by distributing prayer-focused resources (articles, books, and so on) to various leaders and members to stir up their interest for daily prayer.
- *Weekly* – We usually held an all-church meeting devoted to prayer once a week. In addition, small groups transformed into places of prayer, and leaders were trained in how to facilitate Spirit-led prayer.
- *Monthly* – Some of our members who were unsure about coming to a weekly gathering were willing to try a monthly prayer time. These times allowed people who were hesitant to jump into (what they thought was) the deep end of the pool get in more gradually, wading in at their own pace. These gatherings were often focused on Christ as together we celebrated the Lord's Supper, and shared songs, Scriptures and spoken prayers of thanksgiving.
- *Seasonally* – Often holidays or other special days provided the opportunity to call the church to prayer. These special events varied in theme (such as the National Day of Prayer) or focus (e.g. spiritual warfare on Halloween). We also held prayer workshops several times a year that combined teaching and modeling as a way to help members take another step into the ministry of prayer.
- *Annually* – Soon after our Berlin Wall experience, I (Phil Miglioratti) had begun attending a Pastors' Prayer Group

(nppn.org/PPG.htm) in which we actually spent more time praying than talking! At least once a year we would get away for an extended time of prayer. Those one-day retreats were life-transforming for me personally, but also led me to change our congregation's yearly planning retreats. As the leaders of the church came aside to plan I made certain we also set aside substantial time to pray. We learned that the unity we needed in order to discern and decide future plans was the fruit of spending significant time praising, seeking, and listening to the Lord before and during our planning sessions. Because of the prayerful focus of the few, the entire congregation was blessed with God's agenda for the coming year.

The possibilities are endless when a pastor, prayer leader or church leadership team champions a rhythmic perspective on the prayer life of the congregation. If you would like to begin a rhythm of prayer in your church, ask yourself these questions as you pray, and fully consider the next twelve months:

- *Daily:* What resources can you provide to your church members to challenge and equip them to pray meaningfully every day? What can you do to encourage couples to pray together, to see the family altar restored?[4]
- *Weekly:* Is there a weekly doorway into a place of prayer that is appropriate for everyone in your congregation? Is there substantial time given to prayer when men's or women's groups meet? Do the Sunday school classes or fellowship groups have a segment devoted to prayer? Is there a prayer room available for members to visit any time? Do worshippers have an opportunity to participate in prayer during the weekend services?
- *Monthly:* Can you provide training workshops incorporating a focus on a specific aspect of prayer (such as intercession, missions-focused groups, prayer walking, or healing prayer)? Could you invite the members to the Lord's Table with a different prayer emphasis each month?

- *Seasonally:* Which holidays can you capitalize upon to create a special prayer event each month? For example, Valentine's Day (marriages), Thanksgiving, or the beginning of the new school year?
- Annually: Could you provide your members with a 24- to 48-hour prayer summit experience? (Go to www.prayer-summits.net for information.)

If you can start motivating your congregation to become actively involved in church-wide prayer, walls may come down and all heaven might break loose![5]

Your prayer effort is now public. Your goal is congregational engagement. Get 'em praying. Your first step will be more congregational prayer. Go slow. Yet, promote more aggressively, the church-wide prayer meeting. Offer additional prayer options. Pay attention to the level of engagement, but don't worry specifically about the numbers. Don't abandon the effort because the prayer objective does not seem to be popular. Persist. It is the only pathway to spiritual awakening. Your core leader-learners should be more determined now than ever. So, gently expose the congregation to various prayer emphases – personal transformational prayer, family prayer, intercession, prayer evangelism, and to various prayer themes – prayer for revival and awakening, prayer for the nation, for the lost and the never reached. As you expose them to lost-ness, to the needs of the city and the world, you will discover that information is fuel for prayer fire – and that is the value of your research and discovery phase. The Holy Spirit will open their eyes and inspire prayer.

Plan to take at least a year in introducing various new prayer initiatives and exercises. Look for existing national and international prayer resources that are easily imported and adapted. Don't make the mistake of just filling the calendar with prayer options. Be strategic. Keep thinking in terms of the 'Seven Markers of a Praying Church,' inside of which are the 'four dimensions' – personal and family prayer, congregational prayer engagement, intercessory mobilization, and prayer and mission.

Here is a sample:

- Personal/Family Prayer - Conduct a family prayer night. Do a family prayer revival. Review the resources noted earlier for personal and family prayer.
- Congregational Prayer - Encourage the congregation to pray beyond themselves.
- The International Day of Prayer for the Peace of Jerusalem, the first Sunday of October annually (www.jerusalemprayerteam.org and www.idop.org).
- The International Day of Prayer for the Persecuted Church (http://idop.org and www.opendoorsusa.org), the first Sunday of November annually.
- The Call2Fall Sunday, an opportunity to get a congregation on their knees to pray for the nation occurs on the Sunday nearest July 4th annually (www.call2fall.com).
- Intercessory Prayer. Discover your intercessors.
- Promoting the 21-day virtual prayer meeting in January (www.amerciapray.net).
- The National Day of Prayer unites intercessors and patriotic Americans all across the nation on the first Thursday of May (www.nationaldayofprayer.net).
- The Global Day of Prayer unites nations on Pentecost Sunday (www.globaldayofprayer.com).
- Cry Out America/Patriot Day is always on September 11 (sponsored by www.awakeningamerica.us and www.nationaldayofprayer.net).
- Prayer Evangelism. Great prayer evangelism tools and opportunities are found in:
- The Seek God for the City guide (a 40-day prayer tool used in the season of Lent, www.waymakers.org).
- The International Day of Prayer for Unreached Peoples (http://billion.tv/networking/prayer/) is the last Sunday of October annually.

- A gathering of youth at their schools around the flag pole occurs on the 4th Wednesday in September each year (www.syatp.com).

Integrate prayer opportunities into the life of the church regularly, and systematically – family prayer engagement, intercession, prayer evangelism, the congregation praying corporately. Community prayer.

DISCOVERY MOMENT: Watch the video "The Praying Church."

CHECK POINT!

In this year of offering multiple opportunities to pray as a congregation, you will be able to measure the appetite of your members for prayer. THESE ACTIVITIES ARE MEANT TO BE MORE THAN THEY APPEAR. You will see their readiness and their reluctance. You will probably experience pushback. You are no longer *talking* about prayer; you are calling the people to *actually pray* – and do so daily, at-home, with their spouses, and about the lost-ness of people around them – to pray beyond their own narrow slice of pain and self-interest. You have declared war against the devil and the flesh. The flash points of resistance are a gift – don't miss them. They may reveal a fear of prayer, a lack faith and misunderstanding of the importance of prayer or the theology of prayer and its place in God's scheme, and perhaps, a deficiency in compassion for the lost. These are your teaching and training cues. You must teach and train into the learning gaps. As you teach and train, you build confidence and

America's National Prayer Accord

Church leaders representing 200,000 churches, 70 denominations and hundreds of ministries signed and issued the 'Call for Extraordinary Prayer.'

In recognition of:

- our absolute dependence upon God.
- moral and spiritual crises facing our nation.
- our national need for repentance and divine intervention.
- our great hope for a general awakening to the Lordship of Christ, the unity of His Body and the Sovereignty of His Kingdom.
- the unique opportunity that the dawn of a new millennium presents to us for offering the gospel of Christ to everyone in our nation.

We strongly urge all churches and all Christians of America to unite in seeking the face of God through prayer and fasting, persistently asking our Father to send revival to the Church and spiritual awakening to our nation so that Christ's Great Commission might be fulfilled worldwide in our generation.

CALL FOR UNITED ACTION

Therefore, we humbly, yet strongly, request all churches and all Christians to join together, at a minimum, in the following five rhythms of prayer:

- by daily spending time with the Lord in prayer and in the reading of His Word so as to yield ourselves fully to the control and empowerment of the Holy Spirit.
- by weekly humbling ourselves before God by designating a day or part of a day for united prayer with fasting (Friday, if possible) as the Lord leads.
- by monthly designating, in individual churches, one service for concerted prayer emphasizing this call, with special focus on its neighborhood applications.
- by quarterly assembling in multi-church prayer events emphasizing this call, with special focus on its city-wide applications.
- by annually participating in nationwide prayer events emphasizing this call, with special focus on national and global applications.

faith; then, as learning gaps persists, continue to teach and train into the learning gaps.

Here is an important, critical principle: The prayer resources and programs may change, but the underlying emphases – the recovery of spiritual disciplines, prayer that interfaces with the harvest, satiating all we do in prayer – that will not change! Programs change. Prayer ideas and exercises come and go. But the underlying philosophy and vision, that does not change!

DO MORE THAN INTRODUCE PRAYER ACTIVITIES – THAT IS TACTICAL. INTRODUCE PRAYER ACTIVITIES AS A PART OF A LARGER STRATEGY!

Phase IV – Expanding Leadership Teams and Long-Term Planning

Milestone Nine: Multiple Leadership Teams

In Phase I, you started a congregational prayer meeting and looked to see who showed up. Your emphasis was on developing key leaders and your prayer meeting was a laboratory.

In Phase II, you cast a broader vision, explored prayer models, and surveyed the congregation's prayer habits to determine the level of actual prayer engagement, all to develop an informed plan.

In Phase III, you stretched your congregational vision. You went wide with your call to prayer, and in the course of the months that followed, you offered a collage of prayer engagement opportunities, in addition to continuing your congregational prayer meeting. As you did in the beginning, you must now watch those who show up to pray and demonstrate interest in some specific focus or aspect of prayer. You offered prayer events and opportunities to launch a prayer process. Activities were not your goal, they were a means to your goal.

Now in Phase IV, you want to engage in specific planning for each of the '7 Markers of of a Praying Church.' The track specific prayer leadership teams will lead along the lines of the 4-dimensions of the praying church. They will not only lead prayer activities, but a process of transformation.

For example, you offered family prayer engagement opportuni ties (Phase III) – and now, you have identified a potential team to lead that effort. You offered intercessory prayer options (Phase III), and now you are more prepared to move forward and formally organize and expand your intercessory prayer ministry. You engaged in prayer evangelism; now you are ready to identify the passionate and the interested, and establish a team to lead that effort.

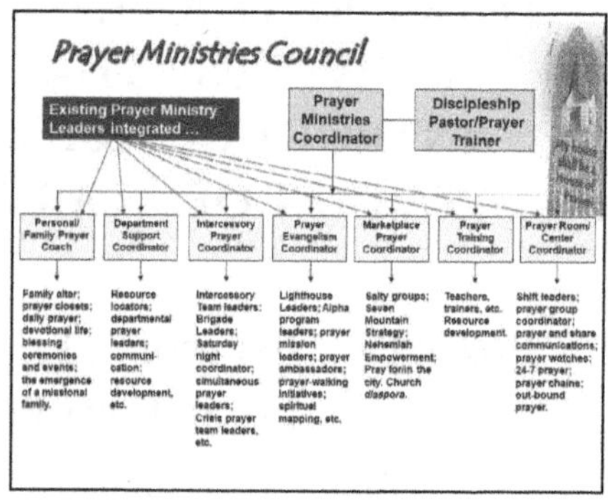

You are now ready now to form and release the teams that will build out the seven markers of a praying church and the four dimensions. In a small congregation, teams may be two-to-three, or three-to-five individuals. In some cases, members may serve on more than one team, and the team itself may cover more than one aspect of prayer. For example, the same team may serve to mobilize intercessors and the prayer evangelism-mission effort. Another team might serve to catalyze prayer in congregational life and manage the prayer room/wall. The leadership team may also be the training team. One team might work on nurturing prayer among families and organizing prayer groups. Be creative, adaptive. Figure out what works for you. Keep purpose in mind, and remember – the path and plan change, the objective doesn't.

The ideal:

1. Prayer Ministries Coordinator
2. Prayer Room/Center Coordinator
3. Intercessory Prayer Coordinator
4. Prayer Evangelism Coordinator
5. Department Support Coordinator
6. Marketplace Coordinator
7. Training Coordinator

Above, you have seven teams or leaders. In a smaller church, this might be collapsed to five teams.

1. The Leadership and Training Team
2. The Family Prayer team
3. Congregational Prayer Leader Team
4. Intercession and Prayer-Evangelism/Mission Leader Team
5. The Prayer Room/Center and Prayer Groups Leader Team

And with only three teams (example):

1. Combine – Leadership and Training
2. Combine – The Nurture of Family Prayer, Congregational Prayer, the Prayer Center/Room and Prayer Groups
3. Combine – Intercessory Prayer Mobilization and Prayer Evangelism

In many cases, the primary leaders of the various components of your prayer effort will be your core prayer leaders, each taking a leadership role in the area for which they have a burden.

Phase V – Engaging the Four Dimensions

Milestone Ten: DiversifiedTraining

Prayer is something we never stop learning. Offer regular teaching and training on prayer, a new class every quarter. Elders and deacons should be trained in prayer – regularly. Every department should be penetrated by prayer – and prayer training.

Prayer training should be broad – personal prayer, praying scripture, prayer and meditation, prayer and heaven's courtroom, the power of entertaining God, intercessory prayer, watching in prayer, lament and prayer, prayer and evangelism, models for prayer, prayer for direction and guidance, prayer missions and treks, there is so much about prayer to learn.

Training objectives:

- Every prayer leader should attend an annual department prayer leader training or in the small church, a church wide training event.
- Train every prayer leader to lead a basic prayer discipleship group.
- Emphasize prayer "learning" and prayer "doing" events.
- Teach in the areas of:
    - ◊ *Personal Prayer* including spending an hour with God; praying scripture; transformational prayer; praying through the Tabernacle, etc.
    - ◊ *Family Prayer* – effective prayer and spiritual times in the home; building a family altar.
    - ◊ *Intercessory Prayer* – what is an intercessor, how to do intercessory prayer, the focus of intercession: the lost! Launch into the deep – touch on lament, the power of watching in prayer.
    - ◊ *Prayer Evangelism* – the need to pray for unsaved people open to the gospel; the plan for prayer for friends and family.
    - ◊ *Theology of Prayer* – prayer as communion with God; prayer as petition – offering our requests to God; prayer as intercession.

The entire church needs prayer training. Offering popular prayer teaching and training only perpetuates narcissism and pragmatic prayer. Quick-fix prayer models, like 'step 1-2-3 to your miracle,' praying feeds the unhealthy obsession with self - and self is what must die for spiritual growth to occur.

When you call for *prayer events,* you discover the degree to which you can effectively mobilize the church. How many showed up when you called a prayer meeting? If they did not come, why not? Have they learned the value of prayer by the experience of answered prayer? *Prayer events* allow "learning by experiencing" the various aspects of prayer. *Prayer training* is for the purpose of application and mobilization for prayer events. No training should stand apart from implementation. Every teaching and training event should be "applied!"

In some cases, such as prayer walks or prayer missions done corporately, or in gatherings of intercessors, you will be able to see the *"learning gaps!"* That will tell you where you need additional training. It may take some courage, but the prayer trainer will have to speak to the *learning gaps.* Avoiding training and teaching in the *"gap"* areas will guarantee the failure of the prayer ministry.

Milestone Eleven: The Family Altar

As one of your first steps, you emphasized personal prayer. That is the anchor of daily prayer at-home. You now want to encourage the expansion of personal prayer to couple's prayer, the family altar, father's and mother's praying spontaneously with sons and daughters, formal blessing events, all moving to missional prayer, out of each member's personal time with God.

This may be fraught with spiritual warfare, the most resisted, the most uncomfortable of your phases. However, on the other side of praying homes is a praying church. There is no praying church without praying homes. The absence of prayer in the home is more damaging than is the absence of prayer in the church.

It might be helpful as a corollary to emphasizing the family altar to call the men to pray together. Freeing men to pray while explaining the importance of family prayer can jump-start family devotions.

The goal is the transformation of the culture of the home to a praying home! Think in terms of seven levels of family prayer.

1. *Personal,* daily, Christ-be-Christ-in-me praying. Focus on transformation in prayer, not merely transaction.
2. *Pray as a couple* together.
3. *The family altar*
4. *Informal Prayers.* Personal prayer moments that are spontaneous.
5. *Formal blessing times.*
6. *The family as an evangelism prayer force.*
7. *The family as a missionary prayer force.* As a family, adopt a nation for prayer. Adopt an unreached people group. Adopt a missionary for prayer. Join prayer support teams when short-term missionaries are sent from your church. Then, pray for the sending forth of a family member on a missions trip, and finally, for the whole family to go on mission together.

As families move upward on the scale of prayer engagement and the family prayer movement expands to and through your congregation, you will experience the power of a 'tipping-point' at every level.

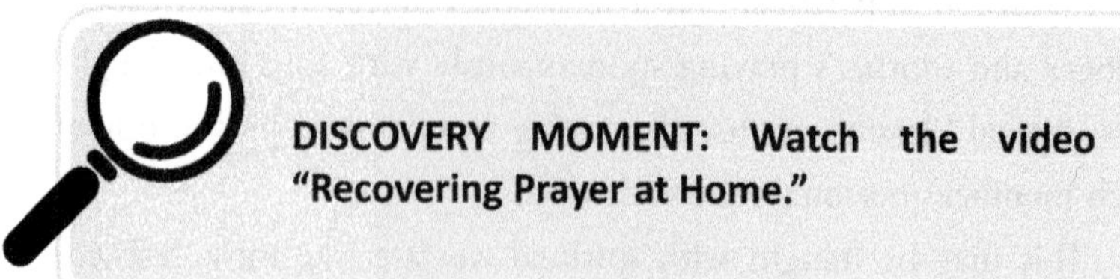

DISCOVERY MOMENT: Watch the video "Recovering Prayer at Home."

Milestone Twelve: Intercession

Intercessory prayer is the critical element in mission. However, intercessory prayer cannot be the center of your prayer ministry.

Intercession is a utility of prayer. It is the edge of prayer, between light and dark, saved and lost, and between inside and outside. It is on the line or the wall, where some advance of the kingdom of God is sought, or some pushback by the Evil One is occurring. It is the means by which God opens closed doors, enlightens blind hearts, opens ears, empowers the witness of an evangelist or missionary. It is fraught with warfare, but its heart is the reconciliation of the lost to Christ. Intercession and intercessors need the tethering of worshipful communion. Mobilize intercessors after you have established an understanding of healthy corporate prayer aimed at transformation, after you have articulated a sound prayer theology.

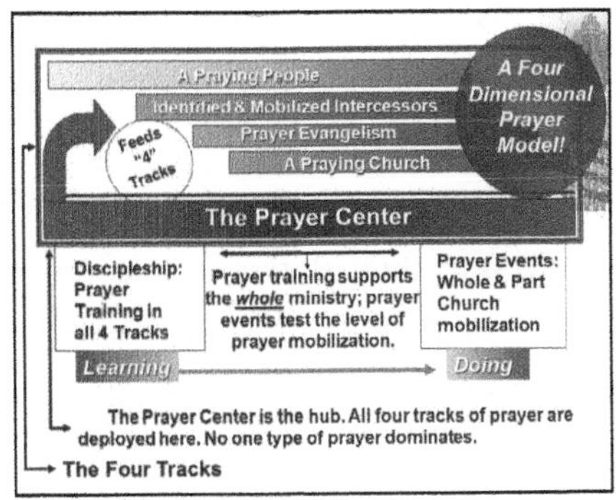

Most people have heard of intercessory prayer, but many have a confused sense of what it is. Some see it as belonging to an exotic handful of the more spiritually elite pray-ers. So they distance themselves from intercession. Some see intercession as a 'spiritual gift' – and they are sure they do not have it and are grateful. There is scant evidence that intercession is spiritual *gift*, especially one limited to a handful of fervent pray-ers. That being said - there does appear to be a group of believers who have a special *call* to intercessory prayer. Estimates are that such Christians compose 5-10 percent of believers. However, all believers are invited into the role of intercession; it is the noblest use of prayer. In intercession, we stand between God and another, perhaps on behalf of their greatest need – to become a follower of Jesus Christ.

Preach on intercession. Teach on it. Identify those who feel a call to the ministry of intercession. Meet with them. Pray with them.

Begin to trust them with assignments for prayer. Debrief them.

Eventually, you want to look at teaming your intercessors into small intercessory teams for each ministry in your church. In addition, for communication purposes, place intercessors into virtual prayer teams of 3-5 or 5-10, depending on your size. These are not intercessory support teams for the ministries of the church. Organize your intercessory effort and stagger prayer assignments in this primary way.

Create a means to convey prayer requests, needs and news to your intercessors through these virtual teams. You might use email, twitter, texting or old-fashioned telephone chains. At times, you may want to do prayer exercises – prayer chains, prayer conference calls, etc.

Milestone Thirteen: Prayer Evangelism

Prayer is at its heart worship, and at its edge mission, and in between God meets our needs. Sadly, far too much of our prayer energy today is focused on our own needs. Not only do we undervalue prayer for the sheer pleasure of being with God, we invest far too little prayer in mission. The prayer ministry of the church is not complete unless it has a missional interface and its intercessors, as well as families and the congregation, is engaged in prayer evangelism. God opens doors by prayer. Any missionary that finds a door of ministry unlocked will, on examination, discover the fingerprints of an intercessor on the doorknob.

Intercessory prayer is posited on the understanding of prayer as communion. Establish worshipful prayer as communion with God, before you develop the prayer evangelism effort.

The prayer evangelism effort is perennial, relentless and ongoing. Every church needs a mission field near – around the church and its facility; and a mission field afar – a nation, an unreached people group, etc. Every member needs to see themselves as a missionary to their neighbors, and inside their vocation network (workplace).

Like intercession, some people are gifted for evangelism, but all Christians should be evangelists – sharing the good news. The goal is every member an evangelist – a 'good news' advocate. Encourage every member to sign up to pray for their neighbors at www.pray4everyhome.com and prayer walk their neighborhood and their workplace.

You cannot see prayer evangelism as exotic. You cannot do it randomly, on occasion, casually – you must own this as a priority. Prayer evangelism is not magic. Don't be unrealistic about results. You are often praying against closed doors, in a nation that has increasingly displaced Christianity, denied prayer in the name of Jesus, and championed pluralism. Be patient. Be persistent. Prayer walk and conduct prayer missions, listen to the Spirit and collect hunches and impressions from intercessors, then narrow your focus, and do another wave of prayer evangelism.

Milestone Fourteen: Prayer Groups

People learn to pray by praying – there is no other way! The best way to learn to pray is with a small group of praying people. Small prayer groups are the best vehicle to accomplish this goal. Form prayer groups, never to exceed a dozen. Organize them around specific themes. Appoint a mature leader to the group. The themes might vary – Prayer for Lost Loved Ones, Mothers Praying for Daughters; Fathers Praying for Sons; Prayer for Unreached Peoples; Prayer for Revival and Awakening; Prayer for City Fathers; Prayer for the Nation and its Leaders; Singles Support and Prayer Group; Witnessing Teens Prayer Group; Prayer for Community Schools; Prayer Missionaries; Prayer for Nations; and more. The presenting reason for every prayer group attracts participants, but the underlying reason is that prayer groups are the places people learn to pray. The small intimate setting with trusting friends invites people to pray aloud. Praying aloud is liberating to prayer. In these groups, those learning to pray are affirmed by veterans. They are mentored, raised to peer status, and thrust into leadership in another small prayer group.

The prayer groups in your congregation should revolve around a healthy all-church prayer gathering. They should not be a substitute for the entire congregation gathered in prayer, led by the pastor. Healthy intercessors are necessary to lead them.

A good goal is a third-to-half your congregation in prayer groups that meet weekly or not less than monthly. This is where you disciple people to pray.

Fearing prayer groups as divisive is a common reason to resist starting such groups. At the bottom of this concern is the absence of prayer group leadership training, and not setting clear parameters. Prayer groups can, and sometimes do, become church plants. If that is a part of your strategy, plan for such eventualities; if not, set clear guidelines from the start. Vet your prayer group leaders.

Phase VI – Maturing the Praying Church

Milestone Fifteen – Establishing the Prayer Room/Center

The desire is for a culture of prayer. The threshold is the integration of prayer into every aspect of congregational life, not prayer as activity, but prayer as natural and reflexive. You have embraced a discipline of prayer that is natural, out of a rhythm of daily, weekly, monthly, quarterly and annual prayer emphases, designed to measure the pulse of prayer in congregational life.

The worship event should now include prayerful pauses, deliberate and intentional moments of congregational prayer engagement. An emphasis on holiness should persistently point to vibrant, healthy lives. An emphasis on intercession should focus on prayer evangelism and mission. A sense of God's love in prayer should nurture lives and create a congregational prayer bond. Worship should be at the heart of prayer. Bearing one another's needs in prayer should be a component. You have developed a prayer room/center, depending on the size of the congregation; and organized prayer groups make use of the prayer room or sanctuary weekly. Intercessors use the prayer room. You have a method, Facebook or otherwise, for emergency prayer needs.

Keep insisting a praying church demands praying leaders. Allow for prayer retreats in the schedule of the staff. Pray together as a leadership team. Make sure the elders/deacons are doing likewise. Insist that every pastor/ministry has a prayer team. Press the importance of pastoral staff and elders/deacons praying with spouses – it is the best insurance against divorce. Model prayer. Let it be the first response to both problems and possibilities.

By now, the core of your congregation should have prayer fever. They have learned to live, not from Sunday to Sunday, but daily, from their time with God, over an open Bible. Your prayer service is healthy. You have identified intercessors. A significant number of your people, by survey, are engaging in family devotions. You have prayer evangelists and prayer missionaries focused on the needs of the community and the lost. The people are praying. A number of congregational prayer members have a prayer closet at home.

Everything needs a place. Depending on your size, create a prayer center (larger congregations) or a prayer room (smaller congregations). Create a prayer counter for information and a way to connect with the on-going prayer effort. Create a focal point for prayer in the sanctuary itself – a prayer corner, a wall, a prayer display, a cross decorated with the names of lost loved ones and prayer needs, an altar laden with pictures of friends and families with needs, especially those who need God. Where, in your facility, are people regularly, visibly engaged in the call to pray? Where can intercessors retreat to for prayer? Where can those in simultaneous intercessory exercises go for prayer? Is there a place where prayer groups can meet not only on Sunday, but during the week? Is the sanctuary dedicated as a prayer room seven days a week? Open and accessible? Made palatable to prayer – lights and worshipful music, or, is it a strange idea that people might come to the church to pray during the week?

Objectives:

- Get the Prayer Room/Center functional.
- Create prayer displays.
- The Prayer Room/Center can serve as a "prayer hub" for the church-wide prayer ministry – with a focus on the city and the mission field beyond.
- Identify an intercessory or prayer group for the day who will come to the church, use the room, the sanctuary, and fill the church with the sound of prayer.
- Encourage "prayer groups" to use the prayer room/center.
- Increase the number of intercessors and intercessory teams.
- Sweep the sanctuary in prayer each week using one of the intercessory prayer teams.

Repurpose the sanctuary as a place of prayer. Prayer Centers typically demand a congregation of a thousand or more. But a church of any size can designate and decorate a prayer room.

The Prayer Room/Center can be the physical place where all of your prayer efforts converge, and from which they flow. Information should be in the room. Displays should reveal the on-going, diverse nature of your prayer effort. The physical space feeds the four-dimensions – personal and family prayer; the church as a house of prayer, intercession and prayer evangelism.

Corporate prayer is critical. Private personal prayer cannot satisfy the need to gather in prayer. And the most obvious place to do this – is the place the same people gather for worship. Make the church about prayer – seven days a week. Don't underestimate the power of praying together.

Phase VII – Forever

This is the forever stage; the 'until Jesus comes' phase. If the church ceases to be a praying church, it is no longer a church. Stay at the process. Let it evolve, but don't chase the exotic. Remember, churches are praying churches because its people are praying people. Don't climb the mountain of prayer and allow the prayer emphasis to be a phase through which the church passed. Watch and pray! In this endeavor, you never finish. You never arrive.

A Simple Overview

1. **Pray together.** Start a *weekly prayer meeting.*
2. **Lead.** Select a small group of *potential prayer learning-leaders* – and begin to meet with them monthly.
3. **Prayer daily.** Emphasize to them and those who attend the prayer meeting, the importance of *daily time with God.*

The above consitutes the essence of the *Praying Church Made Simple,* the first three markers that distinguish a praying church.

For more detail, look to the book:
Transforming Your Church into a House of Prayer - Revised Edition and *The Prayer Trainer's Network Manual.*

4. **Explore and research.** Commit to meet monthly with your learning-leaders for a year. As the group reaches a consensus on prayer teaching and the philosophy of prayer ministry, move from learning to *exploration and research* – "What shall our prayer effort look like?"
5. **Plan.** *Transition from a learning team to a planning team.* Expand your team and conduct a planning retreat with the additional potential leaders. Hammer out your values, mission and vision, a strategy for moving forward with tactical elements.

6. **Lead together.** Transition from a planning team to a *leadership team.*

7. **Envision the church.** Hold a *prayer envisioning evening* for the whole congregation. Go public. Open the process.

8. **Engage the church in prayer.** *Church-wide prayer engagement.*

9. **Expand and multiply your leadership teams** appropriate for prayer. Create a planning-research team for each area of your prayer effort. As you grow your prayer effort, you will begin to hand off the leadership of various components (layers) of the prayer ministry to others, developing a broad, trained, prayer leadership team for each prayer ministry. As you call each segment/department of the church to pray – do special prayer gatherings: youth, leaders and workers, singles and seniors, women. You are integrating prayer into every department of the church. These gatherings can be small, living-room gatherings. Just meet and pray. You are pressing the matter of culture of prayer.

10. **Continue on-going training.** Do at least one class on prayer annually, perhaps even more, depending on desire. Do three in each department.

11. **Organize intercessors.** Emphasize the idea of intercessory prayer to the congregation; the idea of the church as an intercessory community. Preach on it. Teach on it. Identify those who feel a call to the ministry of intercession. Meet with them. Pray with them. Mobilize and team them. Begin to trust them with assignments for prayer. Debrief them. Train them. Do some prayer walking, prayer missions. Hold extended prayer times, for intercessors. Do a prayer chain. Conduct a 24-7 prayer weekend. Encourage each ministry area to organize a prayer team that covers them and their efforts in prayer. Now you can partner intercessors and ministries.

12. **Partner intercession and prayer evangelism** – prayer for the lost, unreached people groups, nations, missionaries. Do it systematically.

13. **Introduce the idea of on-going prayer groups.** This is beyond the church prayer meeting. It presses the issue of a praying culture. It creates more prayer learning engagement options.

14. **Get families praying.** Call the men to pray! And really pray. Have communion. Wash feet. Encourage family prayer. Don't forget the women, but a special focus on mobilizing men will reap major dividends. This helps you launch the idea of prayer in the family.

15. **Place for prayer.** Establish a prayer connection point at the church – a prayer room, a *prayer center,* a prayer wall in the sanctuary.

For more assistance and insight into these 15 milestones, see *Transforming Your Church into a House of Prayer – Revised Edition.* You will greatly benefit by launching a Prayer Leader's Continuing Education Effort.

God bless you on your journey.

The Stages

VISIONING

- Phase I – You are casting vision for the church as a house of prayer, primarily, with a small group of learning-leaders. Incidentally, simply by having a congregational prayer meeting, you are casting vision for the church as a house of prayer. And you are encouraging, daily, personal prayer.
- Phase II – Now, to enlarge your leadership team in order to accomplish your research, you want to cast vision for a discovery process. You will probably do this quietly, at your prayer gathering, and among your learning-leaders, who recruit others to this effort. As you translate research into an informed plan for prayer engagement, you must consider, 'How do we share this data?' – that's vision casting. At the end of this phase, your learning team becomes your leadership team – and someone from among them needs to be able to vision cast in a compelling manner.
- Phase III – This IS your vision phase. You have compelling data – how much and about what you are praying; the history of prayer in the congregation; the needs around you; models of other congregations – it is time to share some of that data, and lay out a plan for congregational engagement in prayer over the next year. These represent the introduction of prayer opportunities, prayer activities – but not the launch of your actual prayer process. In this phase, you conduct a congregation-wide envisioning evening. You recruit team members to help plan and promote the various prayer activities projected for the year.
- Phase IV – Now you cast vision and develop plans for a prayer process in the four dimensions – praying homes, a praying congregation, intercessory prayer and prayer evangelism-mission.
- Phase V – Appoint task teams to lead each focus area in the prayer effort. Each of these teams, working in these various dimensions, will set forth a vision, for example, of praying homes, etc.

- Phase VI – Your prayer room/center, if planned and maintained correctly, will carry forth your prayer vision. People will walk into the prayer room, or view the prayer ministry wall or corner, and grasp the breadth of your prayer ministry vision.
- Phase VII – Cast a fresh vision, and renew the process.

PLANNING

- Phase I – You will need a plan for your congregational prayer meetings. You will need a plan for the meetings with your learner-leaders. See Phase II, 'Resources' for suggestions. Most of your people will need a devotional plan to succeed in daily prayer, that might include a simple Bible reading guide.
- Phase II – This IS the planning stage. Here you do your research and discovery – looking in, back, out, around and up. You need a plan for this research; otherwise, it will only be opinions. Here, from the research, you will develop an INFORMED PLAN, and you will affirm leaders to move that plan forward. They need a plan of action, clear instructions about their role and authority.
- Phase III – You need a plan for your envisioning evening. What data from your discovery-research process will you share? What vision will you cast for the year of congregational engagement? What prayer opportunities will you offer? How will they appear on the calendar? You will want to create engagement teams to help you promote and lead these various prayer experiences during the year. In many cases, these people will emerge as a part of your expanded prayer leadership team, each taking on some dimension of the prayer effort.
- Phase IV – Out of the response from prayer activities, you want to set forward a prayer teaching-training-engagement process. This has to be more than mere activities on your prayer calendar. Your various prayer activities in Phase III gave you a measure of hunger and interest. They may inform your plan for teaching and training, letting you know the base line, for example, of interest in couple's prayer, or prayer evangelism, etc.

- Phase V - Now, you will form leadership teams specific to each of the four dimensions. They will lay out a plan for (1) family prayer; (2) the recruitment and training, organizing and deploying intercessors; (3) prayer evangelism and mission; (4) the proliferation of prayer throughout congregational life. They will work simultaneously toward creating a culture of prayer in your homes and your congregation.
- Phase VI – Now you need a place for all these various prayer processes, these people of prayer to connect. You need a prayer center. That is not merely a room. It should be tastefully planned, for function and inspiration, balanced in all four dimensions of emphasis and you need a plan for its use.
- Phase VII - Chances are, this process has taken you longer than you anticipated. Five to seven years have passed since you entered the process, maybe a decade. By most measurements, half your congregation or more were not members when you started the process. They entered at some stage along the way. It's time to go back to Bethel. Visit the vision again. Relaunch the process.

LEADERSHIP

- Phase I – You began with a group of learning leaders.
- Phase II – In the research and discovery process, you will expand the leadership circle. Quietly recruit at your prayer meeting or through your existing learner-leaders, and perhaps, from your elders-deacons and staff. Discovery and research give way to planning. You will conduct a planning retreat – and at this retreat, you will unwrap your data and forge a plan for moving forward. Now, you need another expansion of your leadership team. At the very least, you need key leaders exposed and informed about your intent to transform the church into a house of prayer. The last step in Phase II is the empowerment of a core, prayer leadership team.
- Phase III - Now you will again recruit leaders, this time, more openly – from the entire congregation. In an envisioning evening, you will cast vision for the church to become a house of

prayer, bringing prayer to the center of all you do. As you share some of the data and dreams, you will find some folks drawn to one aspect of your prayer plan more than others. They will become leaders to help with the prayer activities that you plan for congregational engagement.

- Phase IV – You spent a year, perhaps, doing various prayer activities – but you have not launched a specific strategic process, for example, for family prayer. Now, you want to move each of the four dimensions forward. Those who worked on the various prayer activity initiatives or bubbled to the surface as you did, for example, prayer evangelism may become team members to move that dimension of prayer forward. You have a primary prayer coordinator. Around that person, you have a core leadership team. Each of them may serve as the leader of a specific process, prayer ministry or as a prayer pastor over one of the four dimenions (spheres) of prayer.
- Phase V - Now you want to move forward, simultaneously, in the four dimensions of prayer – not merely advocating prayer resources and activities, but discipling in prayer. That requires, from your core, a broader leadership team.
- Phase VI – Prayer leaders collaborate to establish a prayer office, a prayer room/center.
- Phase VII – It's time to begin again. Envision fresh leaders. Raise up a new generation.

ACTION STEP: Complete the Rating Sheet: Ten Long Term Markers.

On Thursday, December 14, 2005, the San Francisco Chronicle carried a story that reflected the intrigue of the city. A humpback whale had become entangled in web of crab traps and their lines. Weighted down by hundreds of pounds and bound by the ropes, she was struggling to come up for air. Ropes encircled her body, her tail and a line tugged at her mouth. She was alive, but a captive. A fisherman spotted her on the east side of the Farralone Islands, just outside the famed Golden Gate Bridge. A rescue team was dispatched, but when they arrived and assessed the dangerous situation, they determined the only way to save the whale was for the divers to submerge, come alongside the whale, cut and untangle the jumbled mass of ropes. She was massive and distraught, agitated and unpredictable. One shift smack of her tail could be fatal. Divers braved the possible peril and for hours, they encircled her, cutting and untangling lines. The diver who worked about her head, cutting the rope that had snared her mouth said that her eye followed his every move. Suddenly, she was free. What followed was a spectacle none could have predicted. She swam in joyous circles as if celebrating. And then, mysteriously, she returned to each diver, each one, and nudged them gently as if she were thanking them.

The mission you have undertaken is huge. You are attempting, by the grace of empowerment of the Holy Spirit, to free a church entangled in religion. Your mission is fraught with the dangers of spiritual warfare. If you succeed, there will be a great celebration. It will be the most fulfilling accomplishment of your life. What choice do we have? The church, according to Jesus is to be a house of prayer for the nations! We must try to reform the church!

---

1 Chip Heath and Dan Heath, *Made to Stick: Why Some Ideas Survive and Others Die* (New York: Random House, 2007), 25.

2 This process is adapted from the book, *Milestones – Markers on the Journey*

Toward Becoming a House of Prayer, available from www.alivepublications.org.

3 Erroll Hulse, "The Vital Place of the Prayer Meeting." See: www.christbible-church.org.

4 Our Daily Bread is a timeless treasure for daily devotions. Dennis and Barbara Rainey have produced a wonderful book, Moments Together for Couples, with 365 devotions geared for the couple.

5 Phil Miglioratti, *Developing A Yearly Rhythm for Church Prayer* <www.nppn.org/Articles/Article070.htm>.

6 Chip Heath and Dan Heath, *Switch: How to Change Things When Change is Hard* (New York: Broadway, 2010), 134.

7 Chip Heath and Dan Heath, *Switch: How to Change Things When Change is Hard,* 144.

8 Seth Godin, *The Dip: A Little Book that Teaches You When to Quit and When to Stick* (London: Portfolio, The Penguin Group, 2007), 19.

DEFINITIONS

24/7: Prayer, 24 hours a day, seven days a week. This can be seasonal or permanent. A church of a thousand or more is usually required to sustain this level of prayer intensity.

Architect: A member of the Prayer Leadership Planning Team or a consultant/coach who helps with critical, strategic thinking in the design of your prayer process.

Church-wide Prayer Meeting: The call to the entire congregation to gather for prayer, typically, under the pastor's leadership to seek not only the 'hand' of God, but also the 'face' of God. This is not a leadership or intercessory prayer gathering, but an every member prayer gathering with a focus on standing before God and hearing God as a congregation. Scripture-based prayer is encouraged, moving to missional prayer, without forgetting prayer requests and personal needs. This is Milestone One in the process. Call the entire church to gather to pray.

Core Leaders: This is essentially the same as your Strategic Prayer Leadership Team. These 3-5 leaders are the driving force of your prayer ministry effort. Up until Milestone Six, all your 'leaders' should be 'learners.' They assist with discovery-research and in developing a congregational prayer ministry plan. That assures vetted 'core' leaders who agree with the mission and vision, the values and strategic process. At Milestone Six, you affirm them and other leaders around them.

Church-wide Enlistment: A further stage in the growth of your prayer effort. It occurs late in Phase III, at Milestone Eight. Prior to this point, you should be selective in recruiting prayer learner-leaders and those who assist with research and planning. With a vetted, stable core of leaders, you are ready to invite members from the congregation, not merely to pray together – you have been doing that – but to assist in leading some aspect of the prayer effort.

Discovery Process: This is Phase II, Milestone Four. This is the research phase. This phase will take at least three months of intensive involvement. You will need to expand your leadership team during this process, bringing around your SLT a group to help with the discovery/research process. You will need survey instruments to measure prayer and prayer interest in the congregation. You will be well served to pay for a mission profile of your community (Contact PROJECT PRAY for more information, 855-842-5483). You need hard data on your harvest field and your harvest force.

Envisioning Evening: This is a tool for church-wide enlistment. On this evening, or a series of evenings, you will invite the congregation to a prayer vision event. You will attract those interested in involvement in your prayer process. You will share the vision and mission for prayer, data from your discovery/research process, and ideas for moving forward. You will recruit volunteers to specific focus areas and from them form implementation/event planning teams.

Ethos: Refers to the 'culture' of the church, not the tangibles or new tools, not to ministry techniques and practical ideas, but to the environment in which they are implemented – the levels of grace and love, kindness and forgiveness, the 'spirit' of the teams. Prayer *praxis* is not adequate; we must change the culture of our churches and leadership teams.

Focus Areas: Focus areas are the micro areas of prayer. They are tied, to an extent, to the four dimensions and the Seven Markers of a Praying Church. Each focus area – personal and family prayer; intercessory prayer; prayer evangelism; marketplace prayer; the prayer room/center, and even specializations like children, youth/teen prayer, singles, seniors, etc. – will need a leadership team.

Implementation Team: Essentially the same as 'task teams' who are either leading a 'focus area' and developing a plan for that specific area or planning and leading an event, whether it is a learning or doing event. Implementers begin their work in Phase III, at Milestone Eight, as you begin to unwrap prayer events and opportunities in the congregation, testing interest on different fronts. The 'permanent' leadership teams are formed in Phase IV at Milestone Nine.

Intercessors: All believers are charged with the ministry of intercessor, tied to reconciliation. Intercession does not appear to be a spiritual gift, but there are often in a congregation, a small group, who are hard-core intercessors. They usually comprise five-percent of the congregation, no more than ten-percent. Identifying them, teaming and directing them, debriefing and affirming them, can often spark a spirit of intercession in the whole of the church. Intercessors are identified and organized in Phase V, at Milestone Twelve.

Intercessory Prayer Meeting: This is a gathering of intercessors to intercede. It is not the church wide gathering. It is transactional, missional prayer. It often tends to be more intense than the church wide prayer meeting.

Learning Team/Learning Leader Team: In the early going, you build a leadership team by building a learning team. Insist that in the area of prayer, everyone is a learner. Humility is critical to unity. Your initial team will remain a learning team through the first year, meeting to pray and review learning materials. They will evolve into a discovery/research team, then a planning team, and finally, their leadership will be affirmed.

Milestones: Measures of progress in the journey to make a church a house of prayer for the nations. There are fifteen Milestones, unwrapped in seven Phases, typically over a 5-year period in a congregation. Some of the milestones are unwrapped simultaneously, others, sequentially. These are the basis of the book, *Milestones – Markers on the Journey Toward Becoming a House of Prayer,* by PROJECT PRAY. An overview is found in the book, *Transforming Your Church into a House of Prayer – Revised Edition;* and, the first three milestones are the subject of the book, *The Praying Church Made Simple.*

Micro Teams: These teams lead pieces of the larger prayer ministry. They are also referred to as implementers or task teams. They may be responsible for one project or they may become permanent.

Mission: A prayer mission statement is a concise declaration who, what is being done, and for what purpose, with what outcome in view. The mission statement declares what you are called to do, that is, what you 'should do,' where you are going. It is a declaration of organizational direction.

Multiple Leadership Teams: At the heart of your effort is your SPLT, and your Core Leaders, but around them, perhaps with members of the SPLT leading different aspects of prayer, serving as captains of task teams, are multiple leadership teams. These micro teams carry the burden for some specific aspect of the prayer effort.

Phases: The process of transforming your church into a house of prayer is a multi-year journey. We have divided that journey into Milestones, measures of your progress, and grouped those into phases. In some phases, your milestone efforts are sequential, one following another. In other cases, they are simultaneous.

- Phase I – Learning About and Doing Prayer – The Launch (3 *Simultaneous* Milestones)
- Phase II – Discovery (3 *Sequential* Milestones)
- Phase III – Going Public: Feeding the Prayer Fire and Finding Leaders (2 *Sequential* Milestones)

- Phase IV – Expanding Leadership Teams and Long Term Planning (2 *Sequential* Milestones)
- Phase V – Engaging the Four Dimensions (4 *Simultaneous* Milestones)
- Phase VI – Maturing the Praying Church (1 Milestone)
- Phase VII – Forever – Repeat the Cycle with new leaders!

Prayer Council/Prayer Ministries Council: Your Prayer Council is every prayer ministry leader in your congregation.

Prayer Implementation Plan/Strategy: Out of your research and discovery, and using this resources, perhaps with others recommended, such as *The Praying Church Made Simple* and *Milestones – Markers on the Journey Toward Becoming a House of Prayer,* you want to project a multi-year implementation strategy, a big picture plan. Of course, it will be revised, perhaps, numerous times, but this is your blueprint for moving forward.

Prayer Force: The sum total of your prayer efforts, the full force of people and prayer activities in your congregation. It is leaders and planners, strategists and implementers, specialized intercessors and all others.

Prayer Leader Continuing Education (PLCE): The PROJECT PRAY PLCE is a quarterly gathering of prayer learner-leaders from 3-12 congregations for a two-and-a-half hour gathering that involves teaching, the introduction of tools, and time for each congregational prayer team to 'talk-it-over and take-it-home.' It is a 15 session, 43 month program that is designed to encourage congregational prayer teams in the early stages of their journey to make their church a house of prayer.

Prayer Ministry Surveys: Every church needs to measure the depth of and commitment to prayer by its members and leaders, as well as prayer theology and assumptions. A number of instruments have been created to assist in that assessment process. Contact PROJECT PRAY (855-842-5483) for more infromation. These instruments can be used throughout your journey, but they are particularly helpful in the Discovery phase.

Research and Discovery: In Phase II, at Milestone Four, you enter discovery-research. Here you conduct research on the levels of prayer inside the church. You look back at the history of the congregation. You look for models of prayer. You look around for prayer needs in the community. This is when a demographic harvest field assessment is helpful. This information is critical for your planning.

Strategic Leadership Team/Strategic Prayer Leadership Team (SLT/SPLT): We often refer to this team as the SLT. However, you may have a congregational SLT, and therefore, you may need to add the qualifier 'prayer' – SPLT. This group of critical leaders steward the prayer process. In a small church, what we have called your 'core' leaders may constitute the SPLT. A larger church might demand a larger leadership team. At the heart of that SPLT might be a loosely defined team of two or three leaders, that are the very 'core,' the heart of your prayer effort. The SPLT might also be leaders of micro-teams, implementation teams, that carry on the specific areas of your prayer effort.

Strategic Planning Team (SPT): This team is typically a very small group of strategic thinkers – three-to-five. It may be the pastor, the prayer leader/coordinator and a strategic planner, an idea architect, who knows how to strategically, and sequentially, lay out a multi-year plan that integrates learning and doing, building out the four dimensions and Seven Markers of a Praying Church.

Strategy/Tactics: Strategy is the 'big picture *plan.*' Tactics are the short-term *steps* of that big-picture process – the parts. Strategy is the architectural plan; it guides the contractor. Tactics are subset plans, at times that are a collection of small steps, at others, a single step. This is the stuff of sub-contractors. Tactics push the one domino over – the one program, the one event; strategy lines up the dominoes in order that one program and event leads to another, and that the energy of the one event is carried over into another. Tactics focus on a single endeavor; but strategy aligns and harnesses the various endeavors, noting: this (training) is being done to prepare for that (event/exercise), and that (event) sets up what follows. One failure in the chain and the process is endangered. The architect (SPT) builds in back-up plans.

Task Teams: Task Teams are essentially the same as 'implementation teams' who are either leading a 'focus area' and developing a plan for that specific area or planning and leading an event, whether it is a learning or doing event. Implementers begin their work in Phase III, at Milestone Eight, as you begin to unwrap prayer events and opportunities in the congregation, testing interest on different fronts. The 'permanent' leadership teams are formed in Phase IV at Milestone Nine.

The Four Dimensions: The core of the philosophy of prayer ministry in all of the works of PROJECT PRAY. They are at the heart of the Seven Markers of a Praying Church. The four dimensions are actually two pairs in the prayer process. The first pair is praying homes and a praying church; at-home and at-church prayer. The second pair is intercessory mobilization turned outward in prayer evangelism.

The 'Ragged' Notebook: As you begin your journey, you want to collect, in one place, all the prayer efforts that exist in your congregation. This will include those who lead groups, advocate for prayer causes, etc. It should include formal and informal prayer groups and opportunities. It might include such things as, how many 'Our Daily Bread' resources are distributed by the congregation. Are seniors praying – when, where, how many? Do your teens participate in SYATP (See You At The Pole), a September, public school prayer gathering held in late September annually. This will be invaluable in your planning effort.

The Seven Markers of a Praying Church: Includes the four dimensions – praying homes and a praying church, defined by homes with a family altar and a church with a pastor-led prayer meeting; and identified, teamed, directed intercessors with a definitive prayer evangelism-mission focus – and with those, a pastor-led prayer leadership team, on-going teaching and training, and a prayer room/center.

Values: Values are not the things that you *call* important, but what you are actually *doing!* By doing, you demonstrate the value of the idea. Do you value prayer? Hammer out *idealized* values – what you *should* be doing and how you *should* behave – and chart your course toward transformation as you compare those with what you are actually doing.

Vision: Vision sees; mission feels; strategy draws a map; tactics are the steps to the end goal. Vision dreams of what the church will look like when it is a house of prayer for the nations.

Pray for a Cause!

Banners for your church or event.

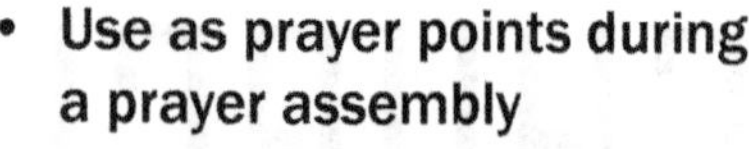

- Use as prayer points during a prayer assembly
- Promote prayer during certain times of the year, such as US Government during election time
- Place in your Prayer Center
- And many more uses!

Banners are available in 3 different sizes:

- Large 30×72 with stand.
- Small 30×48 with stand.
- Petite 18×36 with pole pocket to insert a dowel rod with rope for hanging (dowel and rope not included).

The Project Pray or Church of God logo can be printed at the bottom of the banner for free. Or print your church's logo for an extra $10 for the first banner and $5 for each additional banner.

View all banner themes and order online at:

www.alivepublications.org

PRAYER

THE HEART OF IT ALL

Biblical Principles with Practical Models

RESOURCE KIT AVAILABLE

Includes:

- Book
- Personal Study Guide with Group It Section and Daily Devotions
- Flash Drive with Teaching Guide, PowerPoint file and video sessions

Use as a resource for personal growth or as a small group for discipleship study. Includes 14 sessions with support materials.

www.alivepublications.org